DATE			

A Kabbalah
for the Modern World

Books by
Migene González-Wippler

A Kabbalah
for the Modern World

Santería:
African Magic in Latin America

MIGENE

GONZÁLEZ-WIPPLER

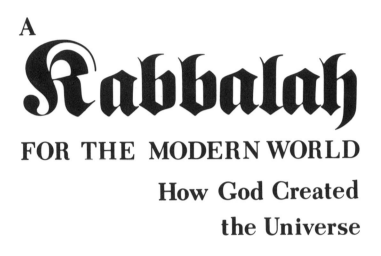

A

Kabbalah

FOR THE MODERN WORLD

How God Created
the Universe

THE JULIAN PRESS, INC.

PUBLISHERS · NEW YORK

Copyright © 1974 by Migene Wippler

Library of Congress Catalog Card Number: 74-75419
ISBN 087097-062-3

Published by The Julian Press, Inc.
150 Fifth Avenue, New York, N.Y. 10011

Book jacket illustration: The Garden of Eden before the
Fall, illustration from *The Golden Dawn* by Israel Regardie,
3rd revised edition, Llewellyn Publications, St. Paul,
Minnesota.

To ALPHA
and OMEGA:
with LOVE

Dear Reader:

This is a book about God. . . .

Contents

Plates

Tables

A Kabbalah

for the Modern World

What is Kabbalah?

The word Kabbalah is a derivation of the Hebrew root KBL (Kibel), which means "to receive." It aptly describes the ancient tradition of "receiving" the secret doctrine orally.

The Kabbalah is a philosophical and theosophical system that was originally designed to answer man's eternal questions on the nature of God and of the universe, and the ultimate destiny of mankind. As a practical system, it is based on the numerical correspondences between the various aspects of human life and the universal laws.

1 The Creation

"In the beginning God created the heaven and the earth. . . ." This is the opening sentence of the Book of Genesis, according to the King James Version of the Bible. The familiar words have been part of the heritage of mankind for countless centuries. Upon their reverberating echoes have been built religions and empires. The ancient words were even heard across the vacuum of interstellar space when man first walked on the moon. Yet Hebrew scholars and Kabbalists claim that these words, revered and cherished by so many, for so long, are essentially false. They contend that the original Hebrew in which the Scriptures were actually written has been hopelessly misinterpreted by translators, and that the real message is of far greater spiritual significance and psychological impact.

Genesis means "In the beginning," and is a direct translation of the Hebrew word *Berashith*, which we will discuss in detail later on. Unfortunately, Hebrew became a dead language approximately 500 B.C. What

1

passes for Hebrew today is Aramaic, the ancient tongue spoken by the Jews during their captivity in Babylon and during the time of Jesus.

During their seventy years' captivity in Babylon, the Jews lost the knowledge of their original Hebrew tongue. When they were finally allowed by King Cyrus of Persia to return to Palestine, the only men who understood Hebrew were Esdras and Daniel. Esdras revised the first five books of the Scriptures, known as the Pentateuch and reputed to have been written by Moses. When these teachings were reintroduced into the synagogues, they had to be interpreted by means of a series of books known as the Targums ("interpretations"), which gave a translation of some parts of the Hebrew text into Aramaic for the common people.

About 300 B.C. Ptolemy II, who ruled Palestine after the death of Alexander, ordered that the Hebrew Scriptures be translated into Greek. The work was undertaken by a group of Essene* scholars who lived in seclusion outside Alexandria, and who were the only people at the time with a competent knowledge of the original Hebrew in which the Old Testament

* The Essenes were a Hebrew sect of ascetics and mystics that existed from 200 B.C. to 200 A.D.

had been written, as well as of Greek. The Essene initiates, however, were reluctant to reveal the secret doctrine of the Hebrew faith to noninitiates, and therefore disguised, with the use of similes and symbolical imagery, the mysteries given by Moses. The stories of Adam and Eve, the serpent, and of Adam's rib, which were introduced in the Greek version of Genesis, have no corresponding passages in the Hebrew original. The seventy rabbis who formed the Supreme Council of the Priesthood in Jerusalem, known as the Sanhedrin, and who were not familiar with the abstruse quality of the Hebrew text, accepted this misleading translation as accurate and appended their signatures to it, whereupon it became known as the Septuagint. The Essene translators remained anonymous. Thus since 300 B.C. the Septuagint has been accepted as the correct Greek translation of the Old Testament.

In spite of common acceptance of the Septuagint. many biblical scholars and theologians have regarded its veracity with growing skepticism. Notable among these was Saint Jerome, who even engaged a Hebrew rabbi to teach him the ancient tongue, but to no avail. Saint Jerome spent twenty years translating the Septuagint into Latin. The Latin version became known

3

as the Vulgate and is considered to be one of the foundations of the Roman Catholic Church since 400 A.D. In 500 A.D. the books of the Old and the New Testaments were first published together as the Bible, as we know it. They became known as the Holy Scriptures and have been since then accepted without question by the large majority of the Christian world.

One of the first translations of the Bible into the English language is ascribed to John Wycliff (d. 1384), but the best translation has been that of William Tynsdale (d. 1536), to which the famous Authorized Version of King James owes much of its phraseology. The standard King James Version is generally ranked in English literature with the works of Shakespeare, in poetic beauty and clarity of speech.

In 1515 a book entitled *The Polyglot of Paris* was published by Cardinal Ximenes, with the permission of the Vatican. This book was extraordinary in the fact that it presented the Book of Genesis printed in three different languages. Each page was set in three columns. The first column presented the original Hebrew text, the second column had the Latin Vulgate, and in the third was printed the Greek Septuagint. The Cardinal's intention was to show that the

Vulgate had been "crucified" between the other two versions, but that it was nevertheless the true word of God. The fact that the Vulgate had been the adulterated product of the Greek and Hebrew versions did not occur to the good Cardinal, who nevertheless did the world a great service by presenting it with a rare copy of the Mosaic Hebrew text, which had been zealously guarded for over three thousand years.

It was not until 1810 that a French scholar named Fabre d'Olivet discovered an old copy of the Cardinal's book. D'Olivet was quite a polyglot himself and had a considerable knowledge of several Eastern languages, including ancient Hebrew. It was with considerable excitement that he set out to study the Hebrew text given in *The Polyglot of Paris*. After several years of deep study, during which he compared the Hebrew original with Samarian, Arabic, and other translations, he wrote his erudite masterpiece, *La Langue Hébraïque Restituée* (The Hebraic Tongue Restored). The book is a thorough study of the Hebrew language and contains a complete copy of the first ten chapters of Genesis in the original version, as well as literal translations into French and English. Thus for the first time since Moses reputedly wrote the Book of Genesis, European scholars were able to delve into the mysteries of the secret doctrine of the Hebrews, the true Torah, as the Mosaic books are known among the Jews.

Although the book was very expensive to print, d'Olivet was able to get it published with a subsidy from the French Government, who considered the work of such vast importance that they agreed to pay all publishing expenses, providing d'Olivet would send copies to all the universities and academies in France. D'Olivet did send copies of his book to the various university heads throughout France and requested that they criticize or otherwise correct the work should they deem it necessary. At the end of six years, since no one came forth to question the erudition of his work, he announced that his book had been found free from error and therefore should be acknowledged as totally correct. D'Olivet's work shows without a doubt that both the Vulgate and the Septuagint, upon which the Authorized Version of King James is based, are complete travesties of the original Hebrew text.*

The work of Fabre d'Olivet made it possible for

* See Shabaz Britten Best. *Génesis Revisited.* London, 1970.

modern Kabbalists to reinterpret the Book of Genesis in its true Kabbalistic and mystical content.

The cosmological concepts that are such an intrinsic part of Genesis can be seen, in the light of the original Hebrew text, to have a significant correlation with modern theories on the creation of the universe and the evolution of man.

Perhaps one of the biggest dilemmas in the acceptance of the account of creation (as given in Genesis) by logicians and scientists is the fact that the whole process was completed in six days. That for God a day may last for thousands or maybe millions of years has occurred to many philosophers and theologians, but the answer to the enigma lies in Genesis itself. And the secret doctrine of the Hebrews, which is known as the Kabbalah, is the key that unlocks the mysteries of Creation, as given in Genesis.

The Kabbalah teaches that God is pure immanence. He is the everpervading energy that fills the universe. He is All, and greater than All. His essence is intangible, unknowable, yet the source from which all things are known. In His ultimate manifestation God is light. In Genesis 1:3, when God says "'Let there be light," He is referring to this manifestation. For before the creation of the universe, God existed as the Unmanifested Principle. The purpose behind God's Creative Action was that of willfully manifesting His essence in the physical universe.

Light is a form of radiant energy that has no mass and no electrical charge, but can create protons and electrons, the building blocks of the atom and thus, of the universe. According to Planck's quantum theory, light is transmitted in "whole pieces" or quanta of action, also known as photons. These "whole pieces" of action are nonphysical, and yet they are the basis of the physical world. And despite the intense abhorrence that teleology, or purposive design in nature, awakens in scientists, the photon or unit of light seems to be motivated by a definite purpose. This startling fact was first discovered by Leibniz, who noticed that the photons that form a ray of light always select a path through the atmosphere that will take them most quickly to their destination. In the words of Planck, "Photons . . . behave like intelligent human beings." This observed phenomenon is known as *the principle of action or least action*. It was also Planck who said that the development of theoretical physics has led to the formulation of the principle of physical causality that is explicitly teleological in character. In other words, physics has proved that there is a definite pur-

8

pose behind the causes of the material world, which is something that the ancient Kabbalists knew long before the advent of physics.

The theory of relativity presented to the world a new, interesting fact about the properties of light, namely, that time does not exist in the world of photons. Clocks stop at the speed of light. Even space is an insignificant concept for light because photons can go through space without any loss of energy. Furthermore, light cannot be really "seen." It simply makes seeing possible. It is an unintelligible force whose existence is proven mostly by the phenomena it creates.

Thus by the logic of scientific discovery, we have a concept of light that categorizes it as a force that is pure energy, timeless and spaceless, pervading the whole universe in an infinity of purpose and action.

All the characteristics that science has attributed to light are remarkably similar to those that the Kabbalists, who see God as light, attribute to God. And if we also take into consideration that according to Planck there is a definite purpose behind physical causality, we can say, without stretching either the truth or the imagination, that science has proved the existence of God.

The two most innate qualities of the human mind

9

are intuition and logic. Intuition is the mystical insight that makes a fact known before it is proved. Logic is the process of analytical reasoning that validates intuition. If we use logic to work with, instead of against, intuitive or mystical knowledge, we create a system that encompasses both the three-dimensional world of pure reason and the multidimensional world of mystical experience. Such a concept is not an innovation of this writer. Long before Bacon, and before Aristotle, the basis for this "higher" transcendental logic was given in ancient Hindu scriptures. Unfortunately, the formulas that made possible the use of this system were lost with the passage of time. Nevertheless, the "idea" of this concept persisted. Ouspensky, in his monumental work *Tertium Organum*, says that:

New thinkers again discovered these principles, and expressed them in new words, but again they remained incomprehensible, again they suffered transformation into some unnecessary ornamental form of words. . . . The higher logic existed before *deductive* and *inductive* logic was formulated. This higher logic may be called *intuitive* logic—the logic of infinity, the logic of ecstasy.

The fact that the concept of intuitive logic had been clearly formulated in my mind long before reading Ouspensky underlines the noumenal quality of this higher logic.

Inevitably science must seek in mysticism a new theory of knowledge, particularly the methods of the Kabbalah, since only the Kabbalah possesses a classification system that enlightens equally the phenomenal and the noumenal worlds. This system, which is known by Kabbalists as the Tree of Life, is based on the harmonious union of opposites for the purpose of manifestation. This concept of opposites differs distinctly from the dualism of Aristotle and Bacon. The general axiom of the Aristotelian logic is that every thing has some thing opposite to it. Thus every thesis has its antithesis, object is opposed to subject, truth to falsehood, good to evil. This concept of duality is the foundation of our logic. The essential difference between the opposites of dualism and the Kabbalistic opposites is that the latter are in harmonious balance with each other. Their nature is either positive or negative, male or female. The result of their union is an Act of Creation in itself.

The Aristotelian logic contrasts sharply with the intuitive insight of Plato, who conceived of Creation in Kabbalistic terms. In the *Timaeus,* Plato describes the Creation of the universe.

God, the all-perfect ruler of the spiritual world, though himself lacking nothing, beheld the sphere of non-being, or, as it was to be called later, matter, and found it lifeless, dark, and chaotic. Himself all goodness, he desired all things to be like himself, good and not evil. So he looked to the spiritual world of Ideas about him and framed a material world after its model, bringing down spirit to unite with matter, making it rich and diversified and endowing it with life, soul and intelligence. He created first the lesser gods, the Olympian deities, Zeus, Apollo, Athene and the rest, and after them the beasts, birds, fishes, and land animals, bestowing on each an appropriate soul. Last of all he poured what was left of matter into the cup in which he had mixed the world's soul and from this diluted mixture created the throng of human souls.

The Platonic concept of the Creation of the Universe, based as it is upon the idea of monism, i.e., the fundamental unity of everything that is, is diametrically "opposed" to the dualism of Aristotelian logic.

The Creation

Only the Kabbalah can reconcile these contraries with its fundamental tenet that opposites unite for the purpose of manifestation. This places the Kabbalah in the realms of intuitive logic, that is, the harmonious union of logic and intuition. Having shown that Kabbalah functions validly in the world of "higher logic," we may quote Ouspensky further:

And then, beginning to understand all this, we shall grasp the separate ideas concerning the essentials of the noumenal world, or *the world of many dimensions* in which we really live. In such case, the *higher logic,* even with its imperfect formulae, as they appear in our rough language of concepts, represents in spite of this a powerful instrument of knowledge of the world, our only means of preservation from deceptions. The application of this instrument of thought gives the key to the mysteries of nature, to *the world as it is.*

We have shown earlier how the Kabbalistic concept of God as light agrees in principle with the concept of light, as proved by science. We have also seen that time does not "exist" for light. This means that all events must exist together, before and after their manifestation, in the world of light. All given *moments* must exist simultaneously and may be in contact with one another, even when divided by great intervals of "time." Thus for God, who Is light, all time processes blend together into an infinite sequence of events. This provides a valid basis for the reconciliation of the Creation of the Universe in six "days," or stages, with the Darwinian theory of the Origin of Species. The long process of evolution, which for man is measured in millions of years, was a simultaneous occurrence for God. Moreover, science recognizes six stages in the Creation of the Universe. Genesis says, "And the earth was without form and void." Science tells us that in the beginning the material out of which the earth was to be formed was scattered about in utter chaos throughout the original nebula. According to Genesis, God says, "Let there be light, and there was light." Science states that the initial molecules were set in motion throughout the nebula giving rise to light. This was the *first* stage. Genesis says that the firmament was created during the second "day." Science claims that during the second stage the earth settled down into a spherical shape and the atmosphere (firmament) was formed. Genesis speaks of the creation of land and water and the vegetable kingdom on the third day. Science says that in the third stage, while the atmosphere was still dense, the waters began to settle in the low places. While Genesis speaks of the creation of the sun, the moon, and the stars on the fourth day, science says that the atmosphere thinned out allowing the sun, the moon, and the stars to be seen. Genesis says that great whales and fowls were created on the fifth day. Science tells us that mammals (whales are mammals) were among the last species to be developed on the earth. Genesis says that man was created on the sixth day, and science confirms this by saying that man is the highest form of animal life.

So far I have been showing how the Creation of the Universe according to Genesis can be verified by scientific data. But a closer look at the first two chapters of Genesis, in the light of the original Hebrew text, reveals an evolutionary principle that is of far greater significance than that implied in the nature of God as light. For in fact there are *two* Creations. The first chapter of Genesis speaks of the universal plan *as conceived in the mind of God*. As such this first Creation is only an ideological plan of the cosmos. It existed only in potentiality to be followed by actual evolutionary development. What God does in the first chapter of Genesis is to manifest His essence as the spark of light from which the universe would evolve. He then ideates a cosmic plan for the Creation of the Universe that is to be carried out in an extensive process of physical evolution. The material source from which the cosmos would eventually evolve was the radiant energy that was God's initial *willful* manifestation. Saint Augustine, who was familiar with ancient Hebrew, gives the same interpretation of this "first" creation. He said: "In the beginning God created the Heavens and the Earth, though this was not in reality, because at first they only existed in potentiality of being." Herein lie the deep motivations for Saint Augustine's ideas on predestination.

Thus our universe was preconceived in the mind of God and as such, predestined. From this can be seen that evolutionary development was part of the initial cosmic plan. Therefore, in the light of the original text of Genesis, the Darwinian theory of evolution is a definite part of the Divine Order of things.

The second chapter of Genesis carries out the conceived Divine Plan on the material plane, as the physical universe. This is the "second" Creation. In chapter 1, Genesis speaks of GOD, the Creator, on a mental plane. In chapter 2 the Creator is no longer GOD but THE LORD GOD. Very often in the Scriptures the

Supreme Being is referred to in various ways, such as God, The Lord God, The Lord, and so on. Each title given to the Godhead in Hebrew has a special meaning and refers to an aspect of the Deity. In Hebrew GOD is ELOHIM, the Being of Beings, the Creator on a spiritual level. THE LORD GOD is Jehovah (IHVH), the actual manifestation of the Elohim in the phenomenal world as the first spark of light whence the universe evolved. The meaning of these two names or aspects of the Supreme Being will be described later on in this book.

In order to grasp some understanding of the Kabbalistic doctrines hidden in Genesis it is necessary for the reader to become a little familiar with the Hebrew alphabet and with some of the characteristics of the Hebrew letters. We will study these characteristics in the next pages, and we will also see an analysis of the most significant passages of Genesis along Kabbalistic lines. It is important for the reader to understand the subtleties of the Hebrew alphabet because according to Kabbalists the first five chapters of Genesis were written in code and cannot be interpreted without the proper keys, which are the Hebrew letters. Each Hebrew letter has a specific meaning and also represents a certain number. The numbers ascribed to the letters have no mathematical significance. Each letter, and thus each number, is simply an "ideogram," a symbol of a cosmic force. The interaction between these cosmic energies is taking place simultaneously in the universe as well as in man. The biblical message is thus intended as a means of awakening all our centers of awareness, acting in this sense as a spiritual revelation.

It is an accepted fact that the whole universe is based upon numbers. Pythagoras said, "Nature Geometrizes." And Carl G. Jung went one step further and said that numbers were preexistent to consciousness. He believed numbers were not invented by man, but rather they were discovered, for they always existed. According to Jung, numbers are probably the most primitive element of order in the human mind and are used by the unconscious as an ordering factor. He further stated that it is not an audacious conclusion to define numbers psychologically as "archetypes of order" that have become conscious. Jung's theory of synchronicity, which may be defined as the simultaneous occurrence of two or more "meaningfully" connected events, has a distinct parallelism with numbers. And Jung himself asserted that numbers and synchronicity have always been brought in contact with one another.

Bertrand Russell was expressing the same thought when he said that "It must have required many ages to discover that a brace of pheasants and a couple of days were both instances of number two."

A number is a symbol used to convey an idea, an abstraction. Many scientists agree that all possible knowledge is present in the mind in an abstract form. In the abstract world of the mind there is no time or space, for nothing in it ever changes. In this purely abstract world knowledge is Absolute, and past, present, and future blend together into eternity.

The study of the abstract comes under the jurisdiction of mathematics, especially number theory, which teaches, among other things, that numbers have characteristics and that no two numbers have exactly the same ones. On the other hand, number is also language, a means of communication. Man communicates his thoughts and ideas by using languages based on numerical symbolism. Leo Stalnaker, in his work, *Mystic Symbolism in Bible Numerals,* says that

The importance of numerical symbolism to the ancients perhaps arose from the fact that the letters of the Hebrew language were originally numerals, and the entire Bible being composed of different

19

groups or combinations of Hebrew letters, it came to be the common belief that the true meaning or proper interpretation of difficult passages of scripture could best be ascertained or reached only by resorting to the numerical value of those letters.

The Kabbalah teaches that God created the universe by means of the Hebrew alphabet. The twenty-two letters that form the alphabet are really twenty-two different states of consciousness of the cosmic energy and are the essence of all that exists. Although they represent numbers, symbols, and ideas, they cannot be easily classified because they are virtually all the things they designate. In order to clarify the preceding statement, let us use the following example. Our ordinary languages are sensually derived, that is, they have been designed to express our sensory perceptions, what we see, touch, hear. The word "house" in English means dwelling, the same as "casa" in Spanish or "haus" in German. In Hebrew, the letter Beth *means* more than house. It is the *essence* of house. It is the archetype of all dwellings or containers.

Tradition teaches that the essence of the Kabbalah cannot be comprehended without a perfect understanding of the Hebrew alphabet. Thus to understand the act of creation the Hebrew letters are an indispensable tool. Table I presents a list of the twenty-two letters with their names, their numerical values, the Roman characters with which they are commonly identified, and their esoteric meanings. The Hebrew alphabet is mostly composed of consonants, the vowel sounds being often indicated by a series of small dots underneath the letters.

The Sepher Yetzirah, or Book of Formation, which is the oldest and one of the most important Kabbalistic treatises, says that the twenty-two sounds and letters of the Hebrew alphabet are the foundation of all things. It divides the letters into three mothers, seven doubles, and twelve simples. The three mother letters are Aleph, Mem, and Shin. The seven double letters are Beth, Gimel, Daleth, Caph, Pe, Resh, and Tau. The twelve simple letters are He, Vau, Zayin, Cheth, Teth, Yod, Lamed, Nun, Samekh, Ayin, Tzaddi, and Qoph.

The three mother letters, Aleph, Mem, and Shin, are a trinity from which proceeds everything that is in the world. Mem and Shin are opposite forces and Aleph is the balancing force. They represent Air, Fire, and Water. The heavens were created from the Fire; the earth from the Water; the Air is spirit, a mediator between the Fire and the Water. The three mother letters are found in the year. The hot season was made from Fire, the cold season from Water, and the temperate seasons from Air, which is again a reconciling factor between Fire and Water. Again, the three mother letters, Fire, Water, and Air, can be found in man. Fire was used to form the head; Water was used to form the belly; and Air was used to form the chest, which again is found between the preceding two.

The seven double letters are called double because they have each a hard and a soft sound, and they also have a set of double qualities. Thus,

Beth—Wisdom and Folly
Gimel—Grace and Indignation
Daleth—Fertility and Solitude
Caph—Life and Death
Pe—Power and Servitude
Resh—Peace and War
Tau—Riches and Poverty

The seven double letters symbolize seven directions: above, below, east, west, north, south, and center. They also represent the seven planets, the seven

Table I   The Hebrew Alphabet*

ALEPH (A) Ox	BETH (B) House	GIMEL (G) Camel	DALETH (D) Door	HE (H) Window	VAU (V) Peg, Nail	ZAYIN (Z) Weapon	CHETH (CH) Enclosure	TETH (T) Serpent
1	2	3	4	5	6	7	8	9
YOD (I) Hand	CAPH (K) Palm of the Hand	LAMED (L) Ox-Goad	MEM (M) Water	NUN (N) Fish	SAMEKH (S) Support	AYIN (O) Eye	PE (P) Mouth	TZADDI (TZ) Fishing Hook
10	20	30	40	50	60	70	80	90
QOPH (Q) Back of Head	RESH (R) Head	SHIN (SH) Tooth	TAV (TH) Sign of Cross	Final Caph	Final Mem	Final Nun	Final Pe	Final Tzaddi
100	200	300	400	500	600	700	800	900

* Although there are only twenty-two letters in the Hebrew alphabet, five of these letters have final versions, which also of importance.

days of creation, and the seven orifices of perception in man, namely, the two eyes, the two ears, the two nostrils, and the mouth.

The twelve simple letters are the foundations of twelve human properties:

He—Sight	Lamed—Work
Vau—Hearing	Nun—Movement
Zayin—Smell	Samekh—Anger
Cheth—Speech	Ayin—Mirth
Teth—Taste	Tzaddi—Imagination
Yod—Sexual love	Qoph—Sleep

The twelve simple letters also represent the twelve months of the year, the twelve signs of the Zodiac, and the twelve organs of man, that is, the two hands, the two feet, the two kidneys, the spleen, the liver, the gall, the sexual organs, the stomach, and the intestines.

According to Kabbalists, the twenty-two letters are also archetypes of different states of consciousness, as follows:

1 ALEPH

is the dual principle that represents all that exists and all that does not exist, the positive and negative, life and death.

24

The Creation

2 BETH

is the symbol of all habitations and recepta-
cles, of anything that "contains."

3 GIMEL

is the activity, the motion of contained, limited
existence or nonexistence; it is Aleph in Beth.

4 DALETH

is the archetype of physical existence.

5 HE

is the principle of universal life.

6 VAU

is the archetype of all fertilizing substances.

7 ZAYIN

is the completed fertilizing act.

8 CHETH

is the "enclosure" of all unevolved cosmic energy.

9 TETH

is the symbol of the initial female energy.

10 YOD

is the opposite of Aleph; it is a steady-state,
continuity.

20 CAPH

is the archetype of receivers.

30 LAMED

is the principle of the conscious, connecting link.

40 MEM

is the archetype of the maternal creative principle.

50 NUN

is the archetype of all individual existences.

60 SAMEKH

is the archetype of female fertility, the ovum.

70 AYIN

is the illuminating principle behind the act of impregnation (Zayin).

80 PE

the same as Cheth.

90 TZADDI

is a symbol of womanhood in a social sense.

100 QOPH

is an exalted state of Aleph, transcending the negative or death aspect.

200 RESH

is the archetype of universal or cosmic "containers."

300 SHIN

is the "spirit" of God.

400   TAU

is the archetype of all cosmic existence.

500   Final CAPH

is the cosmic final attainment of individual existences.

600   Final MEM

is the cosmic state of fertility in man, both in
mind and body.

700   Final NUN

is the symbol of interplay of cosmic energies.

800   Final PE

the same as Pe and Cheth.

900   Final TZADDI

is the archetype of womanhood, in a mythical
sense.

Aleph (1), Beth (2), Gimel (3), Daleth (4), He
(5), Vau (6), Zayin (7), Cheth (8) and Teth (9) are
the archetypes of numbers one to nine. These first
nine letters project themselves into various stages of
manifestations always in multiples of ten. That is, the
next series of letters from Yod (10) to Tzaddi (90)
are exalted states of the first nine letters. The third
series, from Qoph (100) to Final Tzaddi (900), rep-

resent the most advanced cosmic state that may be reached by the first nine.

According to Kabbalistic tradition, when God created the universe He used the letter Beth to begin His creation. Since Kabbalistic teachings are mostly based in allegories and metaphors, one must not take them literally, and must search for their hidden meanings in the symbolism of the Hebrew letters. The letter Beth, as we stated before, is the representation of all dwellings and "containers." In this total sense, it symbolizes the cosmic energy as it became contained and projected into actual manifestation. The shell, the "container" of this radiant energy is the created universe. This is the intrinsic meaning of the letter Beth. But let us now look at the opening sentence of Genesis* in the original Hebrew in which it was written, and let us seek its hidden meaning according to the letter code.

"In the beginning God created the heaven and the earth. . . ." The transliteration of the Hebrew characters into Roman letters would render the original ver-

---

* See also the interesting work by Carlo Suarés entitled *The Cipher of Genesis*, New York, 1971, for a detailed interpretation of the Book of Genesis.

sion of this passage as: *Berashith Bera Elohim Ath Ha Shamaim Va Ath Ha Aretz.*

Berashith

"In the beginning." This word is made of the letters Beth, Resh, Aleph, Shin, Yod, and Teth. According to the preceding letter code, this initial word would be interpreted as follows. The "spirit" of God brought into continuous expression the dual principle of life and death, the pulsation of existence, by containing and realizing it in an infinite array of cosmic manifestations.

Bera

"created." There are three letters in this word, Beth, Resh, and Aleph. Its intrinsic meaning is creation, but in a perpetual, infinite sense.

Elohim

"God." This word is composed of Aleph, Lamed, He, Yod, and Mem. It symbolizes a process by means of which the cosmic energy can be brought into realization.

Ath

"the." Aleph and Teth. The essence of the act of creation has now been given. Aleph (1) and

29

Teth (9) are the first and the last characters of the first nine letters of the Hebrew alphabet (see Table I). The meaning of this word is then clear. Through the initial manifestation of the cosmic energy, the first nine archetypes of all existence (Aleph through Teth) came into being.

Ha Shamaim Va Ath Ha Aretz

"heaven and the earth." The cosmic energy is in gestation, and creation is under way. The act of manifestation is dual. For, in the process of creating the external, phenomenal universe, the cosmic principle brings itself also into manifestation. This cosmic principle is "heaven" and the phenomenal universe is "earth."

Thus, we see that the real meaning of the first sentence of Genesis, "In the beginning God created the heaven and the earth," in the light of the Hebrew text, is as follows:

The Spirit of God brought into continuous expression the dual principle of life and death by "containing" it in an infinite array of cosmic manifestations. This creation is a perpetual process by means of which the Cosmic Principle is eternally brought into realization. Through this initial manifestation the first nine archetypes of existence came into being. The creation was dual, for, in the process of creating the external universe, the Cosmic Principle brought Itself also into manifestation.

By the preceding analysis we have reached a deeper understanding of the first sentence of Genesis. We have become aware of a far more urgent message. For we are now able to form an idea of the principle of creation and of the nature of the creator.

So far, we have been delving in the realm of the Literal Kabbalah. This aspect of the Kabbalah is divided into three parts, all of which deal with the hidden meanings of Hebrew letters.

1 Gematria

According to this principle, Hebrew words of similar numerical values are considered to be identical with each other. For instance, the words *achad* (unity) and *ahebah* (love) both add up to thirteen. They are therefore considered to be symbols of one another.

2 Notarikon

There are two forms of Notarikon. In the first, every letter of a word is taken to represent the initial of another word. Thus from the letters of one word a whole sentence may be formed. A very common example is the word *Berashith*, which we have already discussed. From each of the letters of this word a new word may be formed, thus: *Berashith Ra Elohim Sheyeque-belo Israel Torah:* "In the beginning God saw that Israel would accept the law." The second form of Notarikon is the exact opposite of the first. That is, from the initials or final letters of a sentence, a word may be formed.

3 Temura

According to certain special rules, one letter is substituted for another that follows or precedes it in the alphabet, thus forming an entirely new word.

But the Kabbalah has other teachings that go beyond the actual meaning of words, to imply even deeper things. For instance, ancient Kabbalistic tradition teaches that sound is power. *The sound of the Spoken Word.* It was by means of Sound that the universe was created.

The Sepher Yetzirah, or Book of Formation, says

that the twenty-two "sounds *or* letters" are formed by
the voice, impressed on the air, and audibly modified
in the throat, in the mouth, by the tongue, through the
teeth, and by the lips. So strong is the power of the
spoken word, according to the Kabbalah, that the
mighty four-letter name of God, the Tetragrammaton
—IHVH—is never pronounced by devout Hebrews.
The name is usually substituted for by another four-
letter name, ADNI, which is pronounced Adonai and
means Lord. The true pronunciation of IHVH is
known to very few, as it is believed to be a great
secret, and "He who can rightly pronounce it, causeth
heaven and earth to tremble, for it is the name which
rusheth through the universe." IHVH is commonly
spelled out as Jehovah, but it is extremely dubious,
say the Kabbalists, that this is the correct pronunciation of the Name.

The intrinsic meaning of the Tetragrammaton—
IHVH—is "to be," and it is a symbol of existence. It
also represents the four cardinal points, the four elements, (fire, air, water, and earth), and the four
worlds of the Kabbalists, among other things. The
Name may be transposed in twelve different ways,
all of which mean "to be." The twelve transpositions
are known as the "twelve banners of the mighty

name," and are said to represent the twelve signs of the Zodiac. They are IHVH, IHHV, IVHH, HVHI, HVIH, HHIV, VHHI, VIHH, VHIH, HIHV, HIVH, HHVI. The Deity has three other four-letter names, which are AHIH (existence), ADNI (Lord), and AGLA; the latter is a Notarikon version of the following sentence: Atoh Gebor Leolahm Adonai (Thou art mighty forever, O Lord).

The similarities betwen IHVH (Jehovah) and AHIH (Eheih) are very marked. To begin with, they are both symbols of existence. Also, the letter He (the archetype of universal life) is the second and fourth character in both names. Kabbalistically, AHIH (Eheih) is the unmanifested cosmic principle, God before the Creation, while IHVH is the manifested cosmic principle, the Creation itself. This will be seen in greater detail later on, when we discuss the Kabbalistic Tree of Life.

Another powerful name of God, and one by means of which great things may be accomplished, according to Kabbalists, is the Schemhamphoras, or the Divided Name. This name is hidden in the Book of Exodus, chapter 14, versicles 19, 20, and 21. Each of these three versicles is composed of seventy-two letters (in the original Hebrew). If one writes these three verses one above the other, the first from right to left, the second from left to right, and the third from right to left, one would get seventy-two columns of three letters each. Each column would be a three-letter name of God, making seventy-two names in total. This is the Schemhamphoras or Divided Name. These seventy-two names are divided into four columns of eighteen names each. Each of the four columns falls under the aegis of one of the letters of the Tetragrammaton, IHVH. (*See Table II for a presentation of the Schemhamphoras.*)

From the preceding discussion we see the great importance that words and sounds have in the Kabbalah, and how secret messages, often of vast significance, are hidden in the Scriptures. It is also evident that the message of the Bible is vastly Kabbalistic in context.

The next sentence of Genesis that is to be considered here is the first act of creation, where the Will of God first comes into effect by means of Sound. ". . . And God said, Let there be light and there was light." The original Hebrew reads: *Viamr Alhim Ihi Aur Vihi Aur.* The fact that this sentence is composed of six words is significant in Kabbalistic symbolism, for six

Table II   The Schemhamphoras

I

18	17	16	15	14	13	12	11	10	9	8	7	6	5	4	3	2	1
K	L	H	H	M	I	H	L	A	H	K	A	L	M	O	S	I	V
L	A	Q	R	B	Z	H	A	L	Z	H	K	L	H	L	I	L	H
I	V	M	I	H	L	O	V	D	I	Th	A	H	Sh	M	T	I	V

H

36	35	34	33	32	31	30	29	28	27	26	25	24	23	22	21	20	19
M	K	L	I	V	L	A	R	Sh	I	H	N	Ch	M	I	N	P	L
N	V	H	Ch	Sh	K	V	I	A	R	A	Th	H	L	I	L	H	V
D	Q	Ch	V	R	B	M	I	H	Th	A	H	V	H	I	K	L	V

V

54	53	52	51	50	49	48	47	46	45	44	43	42	41	40	39	38	37
N	N	O	H	D	V	M	O	O	S	L	V	M	H	I	R	Ch	A
I	N	M	Ch	N	H	I	Sh	R	A	L	V	I	H	H	I	O	N
Th	A	M	Sh	I	V	H	L	L	L	H	L	K	H	Z	O	M	I

H

72	71	70	69	68	67	66	65	64	63	62	61	60	59	58	57	56	55
M	H	I	R	Ch	A	M	D	M	O	I	V	M	H	I	N	P	M
V	I	B	A	B	I	N	M	Ch	N	H	M	Tz	R	I	M	V	B
M	M	H	V	O	Q	B	I	V	H	B	R	Ch	L	M	I	H	H

The *pronunciation* of the seventy-two names is as follows:
1. Vehu; 2. Yeli; 3. Sit; 4. Aulem; 5. Mahash; 6. Lelah; 7. Aka; 8. Kahath; 9. Hezi; 10. Elad; 11. Lav; 12. Hahau; 13. Yezel; 14. Mebha; 15. Heri; 16. Haquem; 17. Lau; 18. Keli; 19. Levo; 20. Pahel; 21. Nelak; 22. Yiai; 23. Melah; 24. Chaho; 25. Nethah; 26. Haa; 27. Yereth; 28. Shaah; 29. Riyi; 30. Aum; 31. Lekab; 32. Vesher; 33. Yecho; 34. Lehach; 35. Keveq; 36. Menad; 37. Ani; 38. Chaum; 39. Rehau; 40. Yeiz; 41. Hahah; 42. Mik; 43. Veval; 44. Yelah; 45. Sael; 46. Auri; 47. Aushal; 48. Miah; 49. Vaho; 50. Doni; 51. Hachash; 52. Aumem; 53. Nena; 54. Neith; 55. Mabeh; 56. Poi; 57. Nemem; 58. Yeil; 59. Harach; 60. Metzer; 61. Vamet; 62. Yehah; 63. Aunu; 64. Machi; 65. Dameb; 66. Menak; 67. Aiau; 68. Chebo; 69. Raah; 70. Yekem; 71. Haiai; 72. Moum.

is the number usually associated with the created universe. An analysis of this sentence would render the biblical meaning as follows:

Viamr (Vau, Yod, Aleph, Mem, Resh) "And said."
This word represents an act, a volitive projection of power by means of which Will is brought into manifestation. It implies sound. The fertilizing agent (Vau) projects into continuity (Yod) the dual principle of life and death (Aleph) into the maternal womb (Mem) which embraces and contains its cosmic substance (Resh) and starts the gestation process that will bring forth the created universe.

Alhim (Aleph, Lamed, He, Yod, Mem) "God."
The creative, immanent principle in actual manifestation.

Ihi (Yod, He, Yod) "Let there be."
The principle of universal life (He) is encompassed by continuous existence (Yod and Yod).

Aur (Aleph, Vau, Resh) "Light."
The essence of spirit that is the duality of life and death (Aleph) is fertilized (Vau) and expressed in universal manifestation.

Vihi (Vau, Yod, He, Yod) "And there was."

This word is a repetition of the third (IHI) conjoined in cosmic copulation with Vau, the male, fertilizing principle.

Aur (Aleph, Vau, Resh) "Light."

This is a repetition of the fourth word. This repetition is intended and it has a hidden purpose. The first *Aur* is inner light, soul. The second *Aur* is outer light, body. The result of the fertilizing action of the creative principle is the greatest speed of which the universe is capable, which, according to an ancient tradition, is the speed of light.

We see then that the proper translation of the phrase: "And God said, Let there be light, and there was light," should be:

The Divine Fertilizing Agent projected in continuity the dual principle of life and death into the cosmic womb, and started the gestation process which brought forth the spiritual essence of the Created Universe. The Manifested Cosmic Principle was then surrounded by continuous existence. The essence of spirit was fertilized and expressed in universal manifestation through the cosmic copulation between the male and the female Cosmic Principles. This brought forth the Creation of the Physical Universe in the form of a vast explosion of light.

Thus by the pictorial splendor of this sentence we can envision an explosion of light and sound, and therefore of life, through the volitive act of an unknown principle that gave birth to the primordial substance from which worlds and galaxies were formed.

But how does this Kabbalistic rendition of the act of creation compare with the scientific theories concerning the evolution of the universe?

2 The Cosmic Egg

The first scientist who proposed an effective theory of the beginning of the universe was Belgian astronomer Georges E. Lemaître. In 1927 he advanced the idea that the universe was the result of a gigantic conglomeration of matter and energy that became condensed into a huge mass of the approximate size of thirty of our suns. He called this mass the *cosmic egg* because it was formed from the cosmos (universe).

The cosmic egg was unstable and burst in a gigantic explosion that set its fragments hurtling in all directions. As the primeval matter of the cosmic egg emerged from the "Big Squeeze," it cooled rapidly through expansion, and its elementary particles began to stick together thus forming the prototypes of atomic nuclei. During this time cosmic space was full of vast amounts of high-energy X rays and Gamma rays. There were very few atoms of ordinary matter. In the words of astrophysicist George Gamow: "One may almost quote the Biblical statement, *In the beginning there was light,* and plenty of it." This radiant energy, which at the beginning played such an important part in the evolutionary process, eventually receded and was replaced by atomic matter. In the wake of atomic matter came the gravitational force that broke up the homogeneous gas of the universe into huge clouds, which became the protogalaxies. From the condensation of the gaseous material of the protogalaxies, the stars were formed. Some of the gas that was left over gave birth to the planetary systems. The Lemaître model of the universe is known as the "theory of the exploding universe" or as the "big-bang theory."

According to Lemaître's theory, the fragments of the cosmic egg were hurtled outward at different velocities, depending on where in the egg they were originally situated and how much they were slowed down by collision with each other. The fragments that reached higher velocities would gain constantly on those that had low velocities. This would give rise to an expanding universe, in which the galaxies recede from each other at a rate of recession proportional to the distance.

In 1915, Albert Einstein presented to the scientific world his General Theory of Relativity, in which he described the overall properties of the universe. According to Einstein's calculations the universe is spherical in shape, and finite; in other words, it is confined. Einstein based his views on the form of the universe on a system first described by German mathematician Georg Riemann, according to which, three-dimensional space curves itself in every direction in a constant curvature. This means the universe is a four-dimensional analogue of a sphere. A ray of light traveling on the Riemannian-Einstein universe curves back on itself. It can go on endlessly only by going over its same path. Thus we have a view of a universe that is unbounded, but finite.

All the tests that have been made of Einstein's theory of relativity have proved his model of the universe to be undeniably accurate, and astronomers have generally agreed that the universe is spherical.

The only flaw in Einstein's theory was that he had conceived the universe as being essentially static, without undergoing any significant change. The individual components might move about but the overall density of matter would remain the same. This concept did not allow for either expansion or contraction, and scientists were not satisfied. In 1922 a Russian astronomer, A. Friedman, showed that the static nature of Einstein's universe was the result of an algebraic mistake in the process of mathematical calculations, where there had been an erroneous division by zero. Friedman was able to prove that the correct application of Einstein's basic equations led to a concept of an expanding or contracting universe.

These were all theoretical conjectures, however, without any material evidence as to their accuracy. Proof was not long in coming, however, and in 1925 Edwin P. Hubble, an astronomer at Mount Wilson Observatory, discovered that the entire space of the universe, filled with billions of galaxies, is in a state of rapid expansion and that all the galaxies are receding away from each other at incredible speeds.

Hubble based his discovery on the fact that what had been believed to be spiral nebulae (large clouds of gas floating in interstellar space) were in reality independent galaxies scattered throughout the universe. The spectral lines in the light emitted by these bodies showed a shift toward the red end of the spectrum. According to an accepted law of physics (the Doppler effect), when the source of light is approaching the observer, light waves are shortened and all colors are shifted to the blue end of the spectrum. When the source is receding, light waves are lengthened and all colors shift to the red end.

Lemaître was quick in realizing that Hubble's discovery of the expansion of the universe agreed with the cosmological conclusions of Einstein's theory of relativity, as modified by Friedman. Based upon these discoveries, he evolved his theory of the cosmic egg.

The universe conceived on the principle of the cosmic egg can be of two different types. In the first type, the universe starts filled with a very thin gas, which contracts to maximum density, explodes, and then expands into eventual emptiness. This model is known as the *hyperbolic universe.* It lasts through "eternity," at the same time undergoing a permanent and irrevocable change. In this concept of the universe, there is a beginning and a definite end, and "we inhabit the brief interval of time during which the universe deviates for an instant from its eternal emptiness."

In the second model of the universe based on the concept of the cosmic egg, the force of universal gravitation is taken into consideration. If the universe is pictured as being blown into pieces by a tremendous cosmic explosion, it is conceivable that the forces of gravitation that rule the cosmos might eventually pull the pieces back together again. If this were to happen, the universe would be compressed together again, and a new explosion would take place, which would be followed by another contraction, ad infinitum. The result would be a "pulsating" or "oscillating" universe.

Although scientists are not altogether certain as to which of these two models may fit our universe, modern calculations indicate that at the present time the gravitational pull between galaxies is comparatively small as compared with their inertial velocities of recession. It is a case similar to that of a rocket ship breaking away from the earth's gravitational field as it moves away into outer space. All seems to indicate that the distances between galaxies are bound to increase beyond all limits, and that there is no chance that the present expansion will ever stop or regress.

There is another theory on the "creation" of the universe, which does not take into consideration the concept of a cosmic egg. This theory is known as the "steady-state universe" and it was propounded by Bondi, Gold, and Hoyle. According to this theory, the galaxies are gradually receding from each other, but meanwhile, new galaxies are being formed by the condensation of "newly created matter" in the spaces left vacant by the receding ones. This theory postulates that this new matter is created at the rate of approximately one new hydrogen atom every billion years. Even at such a slow rate, this concept does violate the law of conservation of energy, which says that matter cannot be created or destroyed, and therefore it is not satisfactory to many scientists.

Thus, so far, by scientific evidence, we have a concept of a cosmos, unbounded, but finite, spherical in shape, with a definite beginning and a definite end; a universe that is expanding at a gigantic rate into eventual emptiness, as a result of a gigantic explosion or cataclysmic happening that took place "in the beginning," or, in astronomical terms, at "zero time."

But, where did the cosmic egg come from? Scientists answer this question by falling back on the law of conservation of energy. In other words, if matter cannot be created or destroyed, it follows that the substance of the universe was always there, it is "eternal."

The next question that comes to mind is, what was the cosmic egg made of? What was the primordial substance from which the universe sprang? At the present time, the universe seems to be composed of approximately 90 percent hydrogen, 9 percent helium, and 1 percent more complex atoms. As the universe evolves, the hydrogen atoms fuse into helium, and from helium into more complex atoms. (These latter are formed mostly within stellar cores.) If we go backwards in time to the beginning of the universe, the quantity of helium and other atoms diminishes, while the quantity of hydrogen increases. Thus, at "zero time" the universe must have been made almost entirely of hydrogen. This is the primordial substance.

Hydrogen is the simplest of all elements. It is composed of two particles, a central proton carrying a positive electric charge and an outer electron carrying a negative electric charge. As long as the two particles are separated there is a limit as to how compressed a mass of hydrogen may become. But if the electrons and protons are pressed together, they form a mass of electrically uncharged particles called neutrons. This mass of compressed neutrons is known as "neutronium," although astrophysicist George Gamow renamed it "ylem," a Latin word used to denominate the substance from which all matter was formed.

At the time of the "big bang," the neutronium cosmic egg disintegrated into separate neutrons, which in turn separated into protons and electrons. The protons formed became the nuclei of hydrogen-1 atoms. The hydrogen-1 atoms conglomerated to form helium atoms, which in turn aggregated to form more complex atoms, from which eventually sprang the galaxies and the planetary systems. According to the α, β, γ theory, this entire atom-building process was completed during the course of one hour. Scientists estimate that the beginning of the universe took place approximately 15–25 billion years ago; but this is only an assumption based on geological and astronomical calculations. The real date lies shrouded in the intergalactic dust of the ages.

The Kabbalistic Universe

According to the Kabbalistic concept of the universe, the cosmos has a dual quality, that is, it is composed of a positive (masculine) and a negative (feminine) principle, which are balanced by a third, which is the result of their union. This resulting, balancing essence is known as *Metheqela*, and is a perfect analogue of neutronium, the substance of which the cosmic egg was originally made. Just as neutronium is the result of the union of a proton (positive particle) and an electron (negative particle), the Metheqela is the result of the union of the positive and negative principles that rule the universe.

The Kabbalah teaches that the universe is an "emanation" of the divine cosmic principle. The essence (neutronium-Metheqela) of which the cosmos was created issued from God as the result of the union of the feminine and the masculine principles. As such it is a parallel of the sexual act.

Thus the initial proton may be viewed as a form of cosmic sperm that fertilized the cosmic ovum (initial electron) and formed the cosmic egg, from which, after a period of gestation of several billion years, was "born" the universe.

The prodigious concept of a universe created as the result of a cosmic copulation on a divine plane need not stagger the imagination. All we have to do is observe the natural laws around us to realize how everything in the observable universe responds to an essential union of two opposites, a male and a female principle. From the miracle of electricity to the duality of night and day, everything is harmoniously based on a negative-positive principle. And, if as the Scriptures say, man was made "in God's image," the sexual act must be also an attribute of the Creator, albeit on a higher cosmic plane.

In this Kabbalistic view of the nature of man and of the universe, which agrees so completely with the cosmological principles of the cosmic egg, the universe is "contained." (We must remember it was started with the letter Beth-container.) Therefore it has a beginning and perforce an end. But, if we are "contained" in this manner, it follows by analytical reasoning that there must be something beyond the rim of the universe in which we are "contained." In this respect, the Swedish astronomer C. V. L. Charlier has propounded a very interesting concept that has been called the hypothesis of "unlimited complexity." Charlier suggested that,

Just as the multitude of stars surrounding our sun belongs to a single cloud known as our galaxy, galaxies themselves form a much larger cloud, only a small part of which falls within the range of our telescopes. This implies that if we could go farther and farther into space we would finally encounter a space beyond galaxies. However, this supergiant galaxy of galaxies is not the only one in the universe, and much, much farther in space other similar systems can be found. In their turn these galaxies of galaxies cluster in still larger units, ad infinitum.

Although this hypothesis lies outside the scope of empirical science, and thus cannot be proved by observational study, it is a concept that has fascinated many scientists. For, is it so astonishing to conceive that we are a "world within a world"? Several thousand years

ago an Egyptian philosopher named Hermes Trismegistus wrote upon an emerald tablet the following
message:

> True, without falsehood, certain and most true, that
> which is above is the same as that which is below,
> and that which is below is the same as that which is
> above, for the performance of the miracles of the
> One Thing. And as all things come from One, by the
> mediation of One, so all things have their birth from
> this One thing, by adaptation. . . . So thou hast the
> glory of the whole world—therefore let all obscurity
> flee before thee. This is the strong force of all forces,
> overcoming every subtle and penetrating every
> solid thing. So the world was created. . . .

The "One Thing" in Trismegistus's message could be
the description of the hydrogen atom, as well as that
of the divine essence that emanated from God, according to the Kabbalah. What is then this principle, this
force unnamed and unidentified, in the face of which
empirical science stands mute and irresolute, unable
to deny its immutable, eternal essence? What, then, is
the Creator?

3 The Creator

Most of the concepts that man has built across the centuries on the nature of God have been based on the biblical descriptions of the Deity. In the West the Hebraical concept of God has become the most accepted idea of the Divine Being. Man has come to see God as an omnipotent, omniscient entity, jealous and demanding, exacting and severe, a father image of noble countenance and wise ways. This idea of God became more widespread with the advent of Christianity. To the Christians God became the merciful Father, the perfect all-knowing omnipresence, generous and just, demanding strict obedience to his commandments, extolling the virtues of chastity and humility, exalting poverty over riches and deprivation over pleasure. Yet, this vision of a sempiternal, perfect, omniscient, pleasuring-abhorring, age-old Father does not adhere completely to the biblical story. For, according to the Scriptures, God created man in His own image. To quote directly from Genesis: "And God said, Let *us* make man in *our* image, after *our* likeness . . ." (Genesis 1:26) "So God created man in his own image, in the image of God created he him; male and female created he them." (Genesis 1:27) According to these passages, God was not alone when he created man. For he spoke in the plural; he said, *us* and *our*. Furthermore, he created man and woman in "his own image." It is therefore obvious that there were at least two beings present at the time of creation, a male and a female.

As we have already seen, Kabbalists do not accept the standard translation of the Bible. In reference to this passage, they state that the translators of Genesis purposely obliterated every reference to the fact that the Deity is both masculine and feminine. The Hebrew word used to denominate God in Genesis is Elohim. This word is a plural formed from the feminine singular ALH (Eloh) by adding IM to it. Since IM is the termination of the masculine plural, added to a feminine noun it makes ELOHIM a female potency united to a male principle, and thus capable of having an offspring. The same intended misconception is given in the Christian idea of the Holy Trinity: Father, Son, and the Holy Ghost. In the Kabbalah the Deity manifests simultaneously as Mother and Father and thus begets the Son. We are told that the Holy

53

Spirit is essentially masculine, but the Hebrew word used in the Scriptures to denote spirit is Ruach, a feminine noun. The Holy Spirit is really the Mother, and thus the Christian Trinity properly translated should be Father, Son and Mother.

The feminine principle of the Deity is also known in the Kabbalah as the Shekinah, the Great Mother in whose fertile womb the universe was conceived.

The tendency to smother all references to the creative power of a feminine principle is evident throughout both the Old and the New Testaments. God is consistently represented as a totally unisexual being, who persistently denies "his" own nature by creating a whole world populated by creatures of two genders.

The Kabbalah teaches that the Deity are dual in nature. There are a male and a female principle that are evident in all creation. How could the Elohim create man in the Elohim's own image, male and female, unless the Elohim were male and female also? And how could the Deity tell man to reproduce and be fruitful (Genesis 1:28) if the Deity could not reproduce and be fruitful THEMSELVES? And why should the Elohim provide man and woman with a sensorial apparatus by means of which they could derive pleasure from their union if the Elohim did not have the same ability to experience pleasure?

Throughout the Kabbalah there is always the veiled allusion to the creative power of God, which becomes manifested through the union of the male and the female principles. Therefore the idea of sex, so maligned and purposely repressed by the translators of the Bible, becomes, by the proper understanding of the Scriptures, the most sublime and perfect symbol of the Divine Being. For, according to the Kabbalistic doctrines, the entire universe is based upon the principle of sex, that is, the harmonious union of two opposites, a positive and a negative principle, proton and electron, male and female, fruitfully conjoined to create new life.

4 The Body of God

In the beginning, according to Genesis, ". . . The earth was without form and void; and darkness was upon the face of the deep. And the Spirit of God [Elohim] moved upon the face of the waters. And God said, Let there be light: and there was light." (Genesis 1:2, 3) Again, there is a misconception here. For God does not necessitate to "create" light. He is all light Himself. In the beginning this light was undifferentiated, unrestricted. For the purpose of Creation, that is, of manifestation, the light had to be "contained." In order to manifest Himself, the Infinite, unrestrained Light (the male principle) confined His essence within a Vessel (the female principle). The Kabbalists call the two principles, the Light and the Vessel, *He and His Name*. This is the secret of the Elohim, the Creative Principle.

The Infinite Light, as yet unmanifested, is called by Kabbalists, AIN (Negativity). The Vessel that contains it is AIN SUP, *Ain Soph* (The Limitless). The restricted Light that is the result of the union of AIN and AIN SUP is AIN SUP AUR, *Ain Soph Aur* (The Limitless Light). These three planes of unmanifestation are known as the Veils of Negative Existence.

The states of Negative Existence cannot be defined because being as yet unmanifested they are outside the realm of human experience. Thus they cannot be conceived in terms of anything we know. Nevertheless, this unmanifested Negative Existence carries within itself the seed of Positive Existence, and thus of life as we know it.

The main characteristics of the Infinite Light (AIN) is "bestowal.' This trait of bestowal is defined by the Kabbalists as the intention of receiving for the purpose of imparting. But as AIN is unconfined, He does not receive, He only imparts. His will is to bestow His essence. Hence His willful restriction of His own Light in the Vessel of AIN SUP.

The AIN SUP, being the perfect Vessel, has within Herself the desire to receive for the purpose of bestowing. In order to bestow the Light, the AIN SUP restrained Her will to receive, causing the entire Light to depart from within Her. She then became a vacant circle within the Infinite Light, which surrounded Her evenly, also in the form of a circle. A thin ray of light was extended from the Infinite Light and traversed

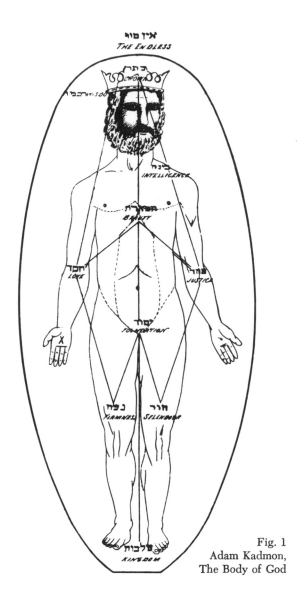

איז סוף
THE ENDLESS

כתר
CROWN

חכמה .500
WISDOM

בינה
INTELLIGENCE

תפארת
BEAUTY

חסד
LOVE

גבורה
JUSTICE

יסוד
FOUNDATION

נצח
FIRMNESS

הוד
SPLENDOR

מלכות
KINGDOM

Fig. 1
Adam Kadmon,
The Body of God

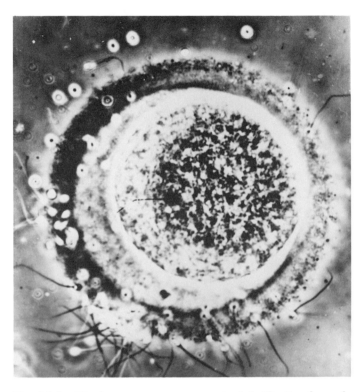

Fig. 2(a)   The human ovum at moment of fertilization by male
sperm (*Courtesy of Landrum B. Shettles, M.D.*)

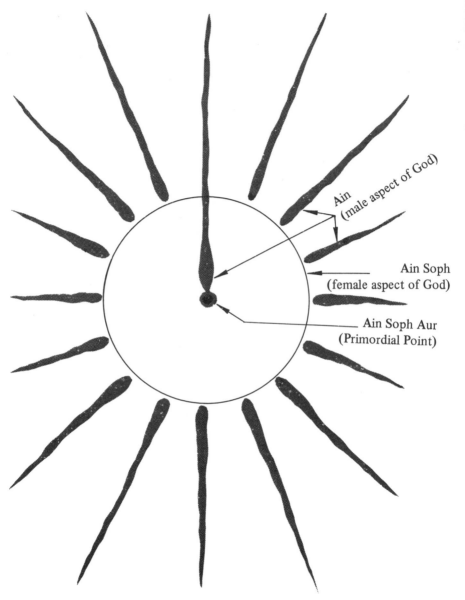

Fig. 2(b)   God, at the moment of Creation

the vacant circle of the AIN SUP, making a series of concentric circles, which are the varying degrees of the entire creation.

The beginning of this shaft of Light forms the Primordial Point, whence sprang the created universe. It is the AIN SUP AUR.

From the pinpoint of Light that is the AIN SUP AUR was formed the "archetypal man" or "world of archteypes," known as Adam Kadmon, or Body of God. This may be likened to the differentiated cosmic energy that composed the cosmic egg at the time of the "big bang," for it had within it the seed from which all the worlds of the universe would eventually evolve.

The Primordial Point (AIN SUP AUR) that traverses the circle that is the AIN SUP is a perfect analogy of the male sperm's head as it breaks through the outer circle of the female ovum. In both instances, the final result is creation, manifestation. In one case, the final manifestation is the physical universe. In the other, the final result is human life (*See accompanying illustrations.*)

The Adam Kadmon is the prototype of man and contains within it the Tetragrammaton, IHVH, which is the same numerically as Adam or man. The "I" of

61

IHVH is represented by the head of the Body of God, the first "H" is symbolized by the shoulders and arms, the "V" is the body, and the final "H" are the legs.

The Primordial Point, which was circumscribed in Adam Kadmon for the purpose of creation, broke through four apertures that are the origin of the senses of seeing, hearing, smell, and speech. They correspond to the four letters of Tetragrammaton, as follows: Yod (I) is seeing, the first He (H) is hearing, Vau (V) is the sense of smell, and the last He (H) is the quality of speech. The four apertures were also the origin of the Four Worlds of the Kabbalists, namely, the World of Emanation (Atziluth), the World of Creation (Briah), the World of Formation (Yetzirah), and the World of Action (Assiah).

The Four Kabbalistic Worlds

Since the eventual purpose of the restriction of the Light was the creation of man, the light that was contained in Adam Kadmon was still too powerful for creation. It was therefore necessary to emanate further worlds in order to veil the light of Adam Kadmon.

The next degree of light to be manifested after

Adam Kadmon was the World of Emanation (Atziluth). The Atziluthic World is the plane of Pure Spirit and is known as the Archetypal World. It is under the presidency of the Yod (I) of IHVH. It is commonly associated with the element of fire. This world gave birth to three other worlds, all in a descending scale of light.

The Second World is that of Creation (Briah). This world corresponds to the plane of archangels and falls under the regency of the first He (H) of IHVH. It is associated with the element of water.

The Third World is that of Yetzirah, which proceeds directly from Briah. It is also known as the World of Formation, and is the plane of angelic forces. It is ruled by Vau (V) of the Tetragrammaton and is commonly associated with the element of air.

The Fourth World is known as Assiah, and is the World of Action, which is the plane of matter and man. It is also the world of "shells," made up of the denser elements of the first three worlds. In this world have their habitation the evil spirits, known by Kabbalists as the Qliphoth. This world is ruled by the last He (H) of IHVH and its element is earth.

Each of these worlds encloses the one preceding it like "the layers of an onion." Thus the Archetypal Man

(Adam Kadmon) surrounds and covers, as "a garment," the Primordial Point of Light that emanates from the Infinite. The World of Emanation, in turn, surrounds Adam Kadmon; the World of Creation surrounds that of Emanation; the World of Formation surrounds that of creation; and the World of Action surrounds that of Formation.

There are four secret names assigned to the Four Worlds, as follows: Atziluth—Aub; Briah—Seg; Yetzirah—Mah; and Assiah—Ben. Again, IHVH is said to be written in a special way in each one of the Four Worlds.

The use of a vast array of names to designate the Deity is characteristic of the Kabbalah. As we have seen, the Bible gives some of the translations of the names as Lord, the Lord God, the Lord of Hosts, and so on. These names are not used indiscriminately or to avoid repetition. Each title or appellative given to the Deity is an exact "metaphysical term," and is used to designate a particular aspect of the Divine force and the plane on which it is functioning.

The Four Kabbalistic Worlds have also been compared to the various elements in Ezekiel's vision; "And I looked, and, behold, a whirlwind came out of the north, a great cloud, and a fire infolding itself, and a brightness was about it, and out of the midst thereof as the color of amber, out of the midst of the fire. Also out of the midst thereof came the likeness of four living creatures. . . ." (Ezekiel 1:4-5) "And above the firmament that was over their heads was the likeness of a throne, as the appearance of a sapphire stone: and upon the likeness of the throne was the likeness as the appearance of a man above upon it." (Ezekiel 1:26) According to Kabbalistic symbolism, the man upon the throne is Adam Kadmon, the Body of God. This figure is the World of Emanation, Atziluth. The throne is the World of Creation, Briah. The firmament is the World of Formation, Yetzirah. And the "four living creatures," also known as the Kerubim, are the World of Action, Assiah.

Purpose of the Creation

The Kabbalah has three categories of ideas on the motives of the Supreme Being in creating the universe, The first category is concerned with the principal reason of the Creator for His creation. This first motive was to make manifest His three basic attributes: Mercy, Justice, and Compassion.

The second category of ideas deals with the intention of the Deity of creating the world in order to benefit man, and bestow upon him His Infinite Light.

The bestowal of God's Infinite Light upon man can only occur when man succeeds in removing the obstruction between himself and the Light. This obstruction is the evil spirit that is incarnate in him. When he accomplishes this he receives the Light as a reward for his effort.

As we have already seen, one of the main attributes of the Divine Light is the bestowal of its essence. But bestowal in the Kabbalistic sense is the will to receive in order to give, to bestow. Man, who is part of the last of the worlds of emanation, the World of Action, is a mixture of spirit and matter. The nature of matter is essentially "evil," and its will is only to receive, never to give, to bestow. Thus man desires only to acquire, without sharing what he receives. As long as man refuses to share, to give, he will be confined in the material world. When he learns this ultimate truth, and joyfully gives of himself, he will vanquish the evil nature in him and will be able to identify with his Creator. The Divine Light that he will then receive as a reward for his merits will be bestowed by him on the Creator because the World of Action is the last of the Four Worlds. Therefore the Light will return to the Infinite Source whence it sprang, forming a luminous circle that will encompass the universe throughout eternity.

The third category of ideas concerning the motives of the Deity in creating the world deals with the ultimate of His intentions; that of revealing His absolute unity, to manifest "that He is first and He is last; that all things are effected by His will alone. That ultimately every curse will be transformed into a blessing and every evil will be transmuted into good."

Proof of God's Existence

To the Kabbalist the best proof of God's existence is the created universe. The creative will is seen in the seed and in the fruit, in the four seasons of the year, in the mating call of animals, in a tender new leaf. To the Kabbalist, God is everywhere. He is in the mineral, in the vegetable, and in the animal kingdoms, always in different stages of differentiation.

One of the most interesting analyses of the Kabba-

listic concept of God was given by Dr. Jellinek*
in his definition of the Deity, according to Spinoza's
ethics. Following is an abstract of the analysis.

1. DEFINITION

> By the Being who is the cause and governor
> of all things I understand the *Ain Soph*, i.e., a
> Being infinite, boundless, absolutely identical
> with itself, united in itself, without attributes,
> will, intention, desire, thought, word or deed.

I. *Proposition*

> The primary cause and governor of the world
> is the Ain Soph, who is both immanent and
> transcendent.

a) Proof

> Each effect has a cause and everything which
> has order and design has a governor.

b) Proof

> Everything visible has a limit, what is limited
> is finite, what is finite is not absolutely identi-
> cal; the primary cause of the world is invisible,
> therefore unlimited, infinite, absolutely identi-
> cal, i.e., he is the Ain Soph.

* Jellinek, J. "Beiträge zur Geschichte der Kabbalah, Erstes
Heft." Leipzig, 1852.

c) Proof

As the primary cause of the world is infinite,
nothing can exist *without* (extra) him; hence
he is immanent.

Macrocosmus Versus Microcosmus

In the Kabbalistic ideology God is seen as the macrocosmus, while man is the microcosmus, God on a
lower level. The Kabbalists despise idolatry, yet they
ascribe the human form to the Deity because man was
created in God's image. But this human form is an
abstraction, a purely hieroglyphical figure. God is a
loving, living, Infinite being, a supreme Intelligence,
cognizant and aware. He is in All, different from All,
and greater than All. His essence is expressed in the
Name that, according to the Scriptures, he gave to
Moses from the "burning bush": *Eheieh Asher Eheieh,*
"I am that I am." A clearer translation would be "Existence is Existence." Existence is "the absolute of reason, existence exists by itself and because it exists."
One may ask, why does a particular thing exist, but
not why existence exists. For existence is the very
essence of being. It is the Absolute. But, since the Ab-

solute is undefinable, can we say, logically speaking, that it is absurd? Not so, for if we could define it we would be limiting and containing it by our reason, and then it would not be Absolute any longer.*

This name of the Deity, "I am that I am," is the first principle of the Kabbalah and has various titles attributed to it, which are quite descriptive in nature:

Temira De-Temirin—The Concealed of the Concealed
Authiqa De-Authiqin—The Ancient of the Ancient
Authiq Iomin—The Ancient of Days
Authiqa Qadisha—The Most Holy Ancient One
Nequdah Rashunah—The Primordial Point

Before the Deity conformed himself as male and female, the worlds of the universe could not subsist. Or, in the words of Genesis, "The earth was formless and void." With the manifestation of the male and the female principle was established an "equilibrium of balance." Equilibrium is the harmony that results from the union of two opposite forces, *equal* in strength. It is rest after motion, counterbalanced power. In the Kabbalah, the term "balance" is applied to two opposite natures, which are equilibrated by a third one,

---

* See also S. L. MacGregor Mathers. *The Kabbalah Unveiled.* New York, 1971.

which is the result of their union. Again, we see here the principle of the Trinity, Father, Mother, and Son; He-God, She-God, and the Created Universe. So were man and woman created, according to Kabbalah, in God's image and "equal before God."

5 God and Sex

The Shekinah, also known as the Matrona, is the female aspect of God. As the male aspect, God manifests as Jehovah. The name Elohim denotes the union of the male and female aspects of the Deity. In this context, we must also mention the great Archangel Metatron, who is said to be the "vesture" of the Deity under His, Her, or Their various aspects.* Metatron may be male or female, depending on the aspect of the Godhead with whom he comes in contact. He is in constant attendance on the Supreme Being, and is the most powerful of the archangels.

The mystery of the Shekinah is one of the most zealously guarded in the Kabbalistic doctrine. Her essence is intensely sexual, and She is said to hover over the marriage bed when a husband and wife are having sexual intercourse. She resides only in a house where a man is united to a woman, that is, where the sex act may take place between man and wife.

* Metatron is also believed to be one of the aspects of the Shekinah.

72

The Shekinah is the Divine Bride, the beloved of Jehovah. From their union as Elohim came forth the manifested universe. It was the Shekinah who walked in the Garden of Eden under the guise of Jehovah, the Lord God. That the Shekinah, who is essentially feminine, may be transformed into Jehovah who is a male principle is explained by the Kabbalists by the fact that during the union between a male and a female there is only one body and one flesh. This is one of the deepest secrets of the Kabbalah, which is revealed only to a select few. From this can be seen that according to the Kabbalah the Divine Being not only have a dual sexual nature but that They copulate on a higher cosmic level for the purpose of manifestation. This explains why mankind was created male and female, why they were given sexual organs and told to reproduce. As Genesis so clearly states, they were simply created in God's image.

To the Kabbalists the sexual act is a most divine and sacred sacrament. Men and women who are not sexually active and unable or unwilling to procreate are considered spiritually barren. A man who does not unite with a woman in this life must return in another life and carry on this sacred duty to his Creator. The concept of virginity as a blessed state is unthinkable

73

to a Kabbalist or to a devout Hebrew. The only virgins in heaven are those who are the handmaidens of the Shekinah, and they are not real souls. The ancient Hebrews placed an extreme importance on marriage at an early age because they believed, as do the Kabbalists, that the marital act brings man closer to God, and that the pleasure that is felt by a man and a woman during their sexual embrace is shared by the Shekinah who hovers over their marital couch.

The Shekinah is called alternately the Daughter of the King and the Divine Bride, but She is also the Sister *and* the Mother of man. She is the architect of the created universe, acting in virtue of the Word that God uttered to Her at the time of the Creation. The Word was conceived and begotten into action by the Shekinah, just like a child is conceived and given birth by a woman.

The mystery of the Shekinah is also hidden in the Ineffable Name of Jehovah (Yod-He-Vau-He). Yod is the Father and the first He is the Mother. From the infinite and divine love that He has for Yod is born Vau, who is conceived, nourished, and brought forth by He. Vau, who is the male child or the Son, has a twin sister named Grace. Of the affirmed union of Vau and Grace was conceived the second He of the Divine

Name. The second He is seen by Kabbalists as a transition from the metaphysical to the physical world, and within it is the seed of the created universe.

The Shekinah is connected very strongly with the patriarchal age. Most of the divine visions that Abraham had were manifestations of the Shekinah, who dwelt in the tent of Abraham's wife, Sarah. That is why Abraham described Sarah as his sister to Pharaoh. Because, as we have already seen, the Shekinah is also known as "sister" in respect to man. She also abode with Jacob and Rachel, and it is said that when Jacob was seeking a wife he "united his intention with the Shekinah." According to the Zohar, when Jacob married Rachel, "he united heaven and earth."

When Jacob lost his son Joseph the Shekinah abandoned him because in his sorrow he ceased to cohabit with his wife. Not until Joseph was reunited with Jacob did the Shekinah return to Jacob. She remained with Israel all the time Joseph was alive. When he died She departed and did not return until the birth of Moses. She is said to have been attracted to Moses because his father and mother invoked the Shekinah at the time of his conception. In Moses' case the intimation is that their union was of a far deeper nature than with the other patriarchs, just as God revealed

Himself to Moses under a new Name (Eheieh—I Am that I Am). It is also believed by Kabbalists that this was the reason of Moses' separation from his wife, Zipporah. This is a peculiar connotation of the Kabbalistic teachings, particularly in the light of the fact that the Shekinah is said to abide with a man only if he is cohabiting with a woman. Another account goes even further and says that the "Holy One of Israel spoused Matrona to Moses, and this was the first time that She made contact with the world below." *

From the preceding it can be seen that the mystery of the Shekinah is the mystery of sex on a Divine Plane. But the Zohar also says that the union between the male and the female is Modesty and Purity. This Purity is symbolized by the circumcision of the male children of Israel. By the act of circumcision Israel is purified and enters under the Divine protection of the Shekinah.

The Kabbalah teaches, as we have seen, that a man who is "incomplete," that is, unmarried or one who never engenders a child, does not enter paradise after death. By paradise is meant in Kabbalistic terms the reunion of man's soul with his Creator. God's com-

---

* See also A. E. Waite. *The Holy Kabbalah*. New York, 1960.

mand to increase and be fruitful implies the procreation of children for the purpose of spreading the Light of God's Name, which is accomplished by allowing other souls to be born and made in God's image.

The Kabbalah teaches that souls descend to the world in pairs, male and female. This is the concept of "soul mates." The souls are separated during their descent to earth. But sometimes, if they are in a sufficient state of purity, they are reunited on the earth.

According to the Kabbalah there are specific times when sexual intercourse should be undertaken for the exaltation and glory of God. For ordinary persons the conjugal relations should be set after midnight because tradition says that it is then that God descends to paradise, and therefore at that time sanctification is plentiful. The "sons of the doctrine," that is to say, orthodox Jews and Kabbalists, should defer their marital relations until the night of the Sabbath, when the Deity is united with Israel. The principle behind this belief is that since God is One, it pleases Him to be in contact with a unified people. Man may be called *one* only when he is united with a woman for the sanctification of God. And both man and woman should think of uniting, not just their bodies but also their souls, in order to blend together with their Creator.

77

Just as there is a specific time preferred by Kabbalists for the sexual act, there is a rule that makes it imperative that the man and the woman should be face to face during the act. This refers back to Genesis when Adam and Eve were created side by side. Only when they came face to face could they unite.

As we have seen, the male must always be united with the female for the Shekinah to be with him. The Shekinah, being a female principle, abides with the woman, and thus, only through the woman can man achieve union with the Shekinah. If a man does not keep this precept, it does not matter how serious and devoted he may be to his sacred studies and religious practices: The Spirit of God is not with him. For this reason the Shekinah is known by Kabbalists as the Indwelling Glory.

The Kabbalists explain this intensely sexual doctrine by saying that there must be a union on the material plane between a man and a woman in order to "offer a point of contact" for the union between the man and the Shekinah. The man is thus said to be surrounded by two females at the time of sexual intercourse; one on the spiritual and the other on the material planes. The blessings of the Shekinah then pour onto both man and woman in equal measure.

God and Sex

According to the Kabbalah, when a child is conceived, the Heavenly King and His Shekinah provide the soul, while the man and the woman provide the body. There is therefore a dual union taking place at the time of conception. In the metaphysical plane that of the male and the female aspects of God, and in the phenomenal plane, that of man and woman.

The Shekinah is said to be in exile, away from Her Heavenly Spouse, since Adam's fall. When Adam left the Garden of Eden, the Shekinah left with him, so that there might be hope for mankind. Thus it is said in the Zohar, the most important of the Kabbalistic books, "Therefore the man was driven out and the Mother was driven out with him." The light of the Shekinah was diminished by Adam's trespass, and thus She must wait until man purifies himself to regain all Her splendor. At this time all the souls will unite with God in eternal joy, the devil and all the infernal legions will become angels of light, and hell will be dispersed. Infinite bliss will reign throughout the universe and there will be Light forevermore.

The secret of the Shekinah and of the Creation of man as male and female is known in Kabbalah as a Mystery of Faith.

6 Kabbalah

According to an ancient tradition the Kabbalah was originally taught by God to a group of angels, who formed a theosophic school in Paradise. After Adam's fall, the angels taught the secret doctrine to the children of man to help them regain the grace of God.

Another version teaches that Abraham received the secrets of the Kabbalah directly from God, at the time of the covenant. The pact was of a double nature. First, he received the knowledge of the Holy Name (IHVH), in which is hidden the entire wisdom of the Kabbalah. And second, he was taught the hidden meaning of the circumcision of male children after the eighth day. The circumcision is a symbolic purification of the body and emphasizes its importance in carrying out the divine purpose. The Kabbalah, hidden in the Divine Name, is designed to awaken the mind and all the cognitive powers latent in man.

Abraham transmitted the secret doctrine to his son Isaac, who gave it to Jacob in turn. The last on the patriarchal line to receive it was Jacob's favorite son, Joseph.

The fact that Joseph had been initiated in the Kabbalah by Jacob (Israel) is seen in various passages of the Scriptures. In one of the most significant parts, Israel transfers his powers to Joseph by asking him to put his hand under Israel's thigh and to "deal kindly" with him (Genesis 47:29). This place under Israel's thigh was the seat of Israel's powers, for therein was the patriarch wounded by the Elohim when they wrestled together all night (Genesis 32:25). Joseph, however, was not destined to transmit the Kabbalah further, and its secrets died with him and thus were lost to the world.

After several generations, during which the children of Israel suffered unaccountable misfortunes by the hands of the Egyptians, the next link in the Kabbalistic chain—Moses—was born.

Moses is seen by Kabbalists as having both a symbolical and a historical personality. He is a symbol of the transmutation of the Hebrew people—from slavery to spiritual freedom. His name in Hebrew is Mosheh, and is composed of three letters: Mem, Shin, and He. The esoteric meaning of the letters renders the "mythical" Moses as a new breath of cosmic life that compelled the Hebrews to break their chains through divine inspiration.

When Moses went to Mount Sinai and confronted the Deity in the "burning bush," he received the Kabbalistic knowledge in the form of God's name: Eheieh Asher Eheieh. "I am that I Am." God then said to Moses, "Go and say that Eheieh (AHIH) sent you. Tell them that Jehovah (IHVH) sent you." Here we see the fusion of the two four-letter names of the Deity, which is the key to the entire Kabbalah, as we will see when we discuss the Tree of Life.*

Moses veiled the precepts and the teachings of the Kabbalah and gave them, thus distorted, in the first four books of the Bible. The fifth book, Deuteronomy, does not have any Kabbalistic traces in it.

The "Unwritten Kabbalah," with all its wisdom and power, was transmitted by Moses to the seventy elders of the tribes of Israel. The esoteric doctrine was then passed on orally through the generations, and thus the secret knowledge was carefully guarded by a select few.

The Kabbalistic tradition teaches that the Torah

* See C. Suarés. *The Cipher of Genesis*. New York.

Moses received on Mount Sinai is dual in nature, for it comprises both "nigleh," the codes of law, and "nistor," the secret mysteries. Moses passed on "nigleh" to the people, but saved "nistor" for the elect.

According to tradition, a controversy developed between the angels and God against Moses. The angels demanded that the Torah should remain with them in heaven instead of being given to man. They contended that since they are purely spiritual beings and the secret mysteries are also spiritual in nature, it was only right that the Torah should be kept in heaven instead of being given to man, who has a gross, material body in spite of the spiritual essence of his soul. Moses pleaded with God, saying that since the Torah consists of, in addition to the secret doctrine, positive as well as prohibitive precepts, which can only be fulfilled on the material plane, it was more proper to give the Torah to man and not to the angels because the Torah is one and indivisible.

The Kabbalistic Books

The oldest book written on the Kabbalah is the Sepher Yetzirah, the Book of Formation. Tradition has attributed this book to Abraham, but modern Kabbalists believe that its probable author was Rabbi Akiba, who lived in the time of Emperor Hadrian, A.D. 120. Heinrich Graetz places the Sepher Yetzirah in early gnostic times. Most scholars, however, agree that the book may have been written at any time between 500 B.C. and 500 A.D., with Rabbi Akiba being the most likely source.

Many commentaries have been written on this short treatise (its length is less than ten pages), but the most illuminating are those of Judah Halevi (A.D. 1150) and Saadia Gaon (A.D. 920), who translated the Sepher Yetzirah into Arabic, with an elaborate commentary upon the text.

The Sepher Yetzirah is mostly concerned with the origin of the universe and of mankind. It describes, by means of the Hebrew alphabet and its numerical correspondences, the "gradual evolution of the Deity from negative into positive existence." The twenty-two letters and numbers one to ten are called "paths," and symbolize all the archetypal ideas that correspond to the manifested universe. Together they are known as the "Thirty-two Paths of Wisdom."

Hebrew scholars believe that the work is the consolidation, by one single writer, of centuries of esoteric Kabbalistic tradition, although there have been sporadic additions and revisions by later authors. There are several Latin versions of the original Hebrew text, chief among which are those of Postellus (1552), Pistorius (1587), and Rittangelius (1642). The small treatise was first translated into the English language by the English Kabbalist W. Wynn Westcott, about forty years ago.

The other significant work of the Kabbalah is the Zohar, the Book of Splendor, which is reputed to be the greatest storehouse of Kabbalistic knowledge in existence.

The Zohar deals with the essential attributes of the Deity, and with the various emanations that issued from the Infinite Light. These emanations form the Tree of Life, which is the kernel of the Kabbalistic doctrine.

According to Hebrew tradition, the oldest parts of the Zohar date before the building of the second temple, but Rabbi Simon ben Jochai, who lived during the time of Emperor Titus (A.D. 70–80), was the first to put them into writing.

Rabbi Simon ben Jochai was a disciple of Rabbi Akiba, who is the accepted author of the Sepher Yetzirah. Rabbi Akiba taught the Torah (the Hebrew

Divine Law) in spite of the persecution of the Romans, until they had him executed for sedition. Rabbi Simon ben Jochai condemned the Romans for their murderous action, and he also was condemned to death. He was forced to flee from Roman persecution, and sought refuge in a cave in the mountains of Israel. During thirteen years he hid there in the company of his son, Rabbi Eleazar. The years that Rabbi Simon spent in this cave were not wasted. "In the safety of darkness, with no text to read, Rabbi Simon drew on the deep levels of memory and vision stored in his unconscious from years of study with his masters of the past."* This was the birth of the Zohar, which was to become the classic text of Kabbalah, the "unwritten doctrine," coming directly from Moses to be finally transmitted to those who were there to receive it.

During many generations, the Zohar was guarded and transmitted by the followers of Rabbi Simon ben Jochai. Then, finally, in fourteenth-century Spain, an obscure rabbi named Moses de Leon published the Zohar. This is what tradition, and indeed, what the Zohar itself, tell us.

* See Rabbi L. I. Krakovsky. *Kabbalah, The Light of Redemption.* Israel, 1970.

Hebrew scholars, however, were not entirely satisfied with the origins of the Zohar as given in the Zohar itself. There was much speculation as to whether Rabbi Simon ben Jochai really existed or whether he was an invention of Moses de Leon. For many years, Moses de Leon was regarded "as the redactor of ancient writings and fragments to which he may perhaps have added something of his own." But many modern Kabbalists believe that Moses de Leon was the sole author of the most important parts of the Zohar.*

After the Zohar was written, it was brought to the Hebrew community of Safed, where the ancient teachings grew and flourished again. Two major trends of Kabbalistic thought were developed there during the sixteenth century. One was started by Moses Cordovero, who wrote several lucid commentaries on the Zohar. The other was the school of Isaac Luria, whose works assumed a "leading position" among Kabbalists during the last two centuries. Luria's writings on the Tree of Life and the eight "Gates" are the most complete commentary on the Zohar. His interpretations are accepted among Kab-

* See also Gershom Scholem, ed. *The Zohar*, New York.

balists as the most authoritative on the Kabbalistic doctrines. So great has been Luria's influence in the Kabbalistic movement that two of the books of the Zohar are based on his teachings. One of them is the Beth Elohim, which is a discourse on the nature of angels, demons, and of souls. The other is the Book of the Revolutions of Souls, a further commentary on Luria's ideas.

The three most important books of the Zohar are:

1. The Siphra Dtzenioutha, or Book of Concealed Mystery, which is the foundation of the Zohar;
2. The Idra Rabba, or The Great Assembly, which describes the mystical "Body of God" in the form of Adam Kadmon;
3. The Idra Zutta, or The Small Assembly, which is a monologue of Rabbi Simon ben Jochai before his death, on the same subject as that treated in the Great Assembly.

Besides the Sepher Yetzirah and the Zohar there are two other books on the Kabbalah that are of great spiritual significance. They are:

1. The Sepher Sephiroth, which describes the evolution of God from a negative to a positive existence;

2. The Aesch Metzareph, which is an abstruse chimico-Kabbalistic treatise.

What is Kabbalah?

The word Kabbalah is a derivation of the Hebrew root KBL (Kibel), which means "to receive." It aptly describes the ancient tradition of "receiving" the secret doctrine orally.

According to modern Kabbalist S. L. MacGregor Mathers, the Kabbalah may be classified under four divisions:

1. The Practical Kabbalah
2. The Literal Kabbalah
3. The Unwritten Kabbalah
4. The Dogmatic Kabbalah

The Practical Kabbalah is concerned with talismanic and ritual magic.

The Literal Kabbalah is divided into three parts: Gematria, Notarikon, and Temura.

The Unwritten Kabbalah is the part of the esoteric knowledge that is transmitted orally and had never been put into writing until recent times. It is closely linked with the Practical Kabbalah.

The Dogmatic Kabbalah may be classified also as the "written Kabbalah," and comprises the various works we have discussed, and others not mentioned because of their obscurity.

The Kabbalah is a philosophical and theosophical system that was originally designed to answer man's eternal questions on the nature of God and of the universe, and the ultimate destiny of mankind. As a practical system, it is based on the numerical correspondences between the various aspects of human life and the universal laws.

The correspondences between allied subjects is found by means of the three divisions of the Literal Kabbalah, especially Gematria. When a Kabbalist wishes to know the intrinsic nature of anything, he finds the numerical value of the name of the subject of his interest by substituting each letter of the name for its corresponding numerical value according to the Hebrew alphabet. By the laws of numerology he then reduces the resultant sum to one of the archetypal numbers, 1–9. For example, if the resulting sum equals 4 2 4, he adds $4+2+4$, which equals 10, which is the same as $1+0=1$. The nature of the subject, then, is to be found in the esoteric properties of archetypal number 1. The essence of any of the numbers may be ascertained by means of the correspondences of the Hebrew alphabet, the Tree of Life, as well as through astrology, alchemy, and various other allied systems.

The law of correspondences is such an important part of the Kabbalah that hidden meanings are found by Kabbalists in words of similar construction. An interesting example is the word "dam," which means blood in Hebrew. This word is "hidden" in the name Adam, which means man. The Kabbalists therefore see a distinct correlation in the union of *dam* and the letter Aleph (A), which is the principle of life and death, the "spark" of creation. They see in the union of A and *dam*, which results in Adam, a blood pact between mankind and the Deity.

From the preceding example we see that the symbolism of blood in the relations between man and God is very significant. This is the reason why men have always offered blood sacrifices to the Divine Being. In Hebrew tradition, all the covenants between the Hebrews and IHVH were ratified with a blood sacrifice, notably circumcision.

Water is seen by the Kabbalist as the potential seed of blood, capable of transformation into that precious life symbol.

According to the Scriptures, Moses changed the waters of the Nile River into blood, and thousands of years later, Jesus changed water into wine at the wedding in Canaan. The correlation between wine and blood is well known. Jesus himself, who is recognized in the esoteric tradition as a master Kabbalist, made this fact obvious during the Last Supper, when he filled a goblet with wine and offered it to his disciples, saying, "Drink ye all of it. For this is my blood of the new testament, which is shed for many for the remission of sins." (Matthew 26:27–28) This "blood sacrifice" is still enacted in the Catholic "sacrifice" of the mass. During the ceremony the officiating priest presents to the congregation a goblet filled with wine and repeats the words of Jesus, "Drink, for this is my blood . . ."

Animal sacrifices also serve to achieve union with God. When an animal offering was made by the priests at the time of the temple, only the fat and certain organs of its body were burned at the altar. By burning the flesh and the fat of the animal the powers of the World of Action were bound. The spirit within the body of the animal bound the angels in the World of Formation. The "higher spirit" bound the archangels of the World of Creation. And the priest's intention bound the World of Emanation. Thus through the act of sacrifice, the Divine essence of the Four Kabbalistic Worlds was united. The Infinite Light would then bestow some of His Light to the World of Emanation, and from there the light would shine to the other worlds, including the World of Action, which is man.

Kabbalistic tradition teaches that prayer and the observance of the Divine precepts serve the same function as the ancient sacrifices. The reason why prayers and sacrifice achieve the binding of the Four Worlds may be explained as follows.

As we have already seen, the World of Emanation is the origin of the other three worlds. Kabbalah teaches that God willed that a portion of His Light, known as "sparks" of the World of Emanation, be sent into "exile" and caused to descend to the World of Action, where they are "clothed in matter" so that man may have the opportunity of redeeming them, causing the sparks to return to their source. For, the aim of creation is that all the essence that issued from the Infinite Light shall return whence it came. Thus when man by means of prayer or sacrifices and the observance of the precepts causes the sparks to return to their source, great "love and joy" are awakened in the higher worlds, and by virtue of this love and joy the Four Worlds are united. This is known as the raising of M'N by man, who then gets M'D (the bestowal of Infinite Light) as a reward. M'N means "mayin nukvah," and represents the "waters" of the feminine or passive principle. M'D stands for "mayin dchurin," the "waters" of the masculine or active principle. The great "love and joy" that result from the union of the sparks (the feminine principle) with the Infinite Light (the masculine principle) is analogous to the pleasure resulting from the sexual union between man and woman, on a higher, cosmic plane.

According to the Kabbalistic doctrine, man's soul stems from God, for it originates in the World of Emanation, which is all purity. Through the original fall of Adam, the soul of man was polluted by the evil spirit, symbolized by the serpent in paradise. God stripped the serpent of its skin, which represented its power for evil. With this skin, He fashioned "garments" for Adam and his wife. "Unto Adam also and to his wife did the Lord God make coats of skins, and clothed them." (Genesis 3:21) The "coats of skin" symbolize the corrupt, material nature of man. The power of man, however, is similar to the power of angels. "It is a Godly spirit which shines in man to help him, when he repents, to divest himself of his own evil, thus to remove this alien garment in which he was dressed because of Adam's sin." For this purpose, from the World of Emanation are extended 613 channels through which the Divine Light is either bestowed on man or withdrawn from him. The 613 channels are also used to "supervise" man's actions in the material world. They are the origin of the 613 precepts of the Torah, which are divided into 248 positive and 365 prohibitive commandments. The body, which is formed after the imprint of the soul, is also composed of 248 organs or limbs and 365 veins. The 248 positive precepts are so many "gates" in the pillar or source of Mercy, while the 365 prohibitive precepts are the same number of gates in the pillar or source of Judgment. When man performs a positive precept, one of the gates in the pillar of Mercy opens and the Light of the Infinite shines upon the World of Emanation, and thence to the other three worlds. Conversely, when man trespasses against a prohibitive commandment, he causes one of the gates of the pillar of Judgment to open, allowing the evil powers to seize hold of Judgment and "visit punishment upon the world."

As we have already seen, the feminine principle or

Divine Presence is known in Kabbalah as the Shekinah. By Divine decree the Shekinah was sent into "exile" to abide with man, until that time when he purifies himself.

When the Shekinah is in Her full glory, she manifests from Her source, which is the World of Emanation, bestowing Her light on man through the 613 channels or precepts. When She is in exile, however, Her light is diminished by prearranged order. The restoration of Her full light can only come through the perfect observation of the 613 precepts.

During Her exile, the Shekinah manifests Herself where the shells or evil spirits abide (Qlipoth). When the diminished light of the Shekinah radiates through the shells, the light reflects on man very dimly, for the shells surround the light, appropriating most of it for themselves. This causes everything in the material world to become defective, so that Judgment increases and gains power over Mercy. This is the reason why there is not enough love and harmony in the world, and in contrast, there is so much sorrow and strife.

When man, by his good actions, purifies himself, the light of the Shekinah is restored and She then bestows Her bounty of light upon man's soul.

The Kabbalistic Truth

The sages tell us that truth, "Emet," is the Maker's "signature." Creation is in principle the "blueprint" of the Creator's wisdom and greatness. Genesis tells us that man appeared last at the time of Creation, the same as a signature at the end of a letter or decree. The numerical value of Adam (man) is nine, the same as Emet (truth). Thus, by Kabbalistic correspondence, they are one and the same.

Tradition asserts that Kabbalah is total truth. Therefore, if in essence man is also truth, it follows logically that the Kabbalistic truths may be found in man. Kabbalah, then, must provide the answers to all the questions that man has asked from his beginnings about his origin and the purpose of his existence. According to Kabbalists, since the Kabbalah is a synthesis of man, it must also embody all the studies known to man, such as biology, chemistry, philosophy, psychology, astronomy, medicine, and so on. The eminent French scholar and Kabbalist, Adolf Franck, said that Kabbalah is the only system known to man that explains the concept of God and the universe both mystically and scientifically.

According to English Kabbalist, S. L. MacGregor Mathers, the principal doctrines of the Kabbalah are concerned with providing a solution for the following problems:

1. The Supreme Being, His nature and attributes
2. The Cosmogony
3. The creation of angels and man
4. The destiny of man and angels
5. The nature of the soul
6. The nature of angels, demons, and elementals
7. The import of the revealed Law
8. The transcendental symbolism of numerals
9. The peculiar mysteries contained in the Hebrew letters
10. The equilibrium of contraries

The Kabbalah teaches that the manifestation of the Deity may be expressed in five phases as follows:

1. Source or Seed—The Ain Soph Aur or Adam Kadmon
2. Root—World of Emanation of Atziluth
3. Tree—World of Creation or Briah
4. Branch—World of Formation or Yetzirah
5. Fruit—World of Action or Assiah

Rabbi L. I. Krakovsky, in his work, *Kabbalah, The Light of Redemption*, states that each phase in this allegory is

the root or source of the phases that follow it. Thus for instance the branch is the source for the fruit, that is, the World of Formation is source to the World of Action; the tree is source to the branches and fruit, thus the World of Creation is the source for both the Worlds of Formation and Action; the root of the tree is source to the tree, branches, and fruit, thus the World of Emanation is source to the Worlds of Creation, Formation, and Action; and lastly, the seed is source for root, tree, branches, and fruit, thus Adam Kadmon is the origin of the Worlds of Emanation, Creation, Formation, and Action.

These five phases form a schema of the Tree of Life, which is the essence of the Kabbalistic teachings.

7 The Tree of Life

Etz Hayim, the Tree of Life, is a glyph, a composite symbol that represents both the Heavenly Man, Adam Kadmon, conceived as the macrocosmus, and man in the material world, seen as the microcosmus. It resembles, in essence, Yggdrasil, the mythological tree of Scandinavians.*

The Tree of Life (Figure 3) is composed of ten spheres known as "sephiroth" (sephira is the singular form). The spheres are interconnected by lines that are called "paths." There are twenty-two paths, which represent the twenty-two letters of the Hebrew alphabet. In Kabbalah the ten sephiroth and the twenty-two paths are known as the thirty-two Paths of Wisdom. The sephiroth are different stages of manifestation of the Infinite Light, and thus of evolution. The paths are phases of "subjective consciousness" by means of which the soul becomes aware of cosmic manifestation.

* See also S. M. L. MacGregor Mathers. *The Kabbalah Unveiled.* New York, 1971.

The sephiroth are known as "numerical emanations," and are representative of the abstract forms of numbers one to ten. Each sephira symbolizes a development and an attitude of the Deity, as well as of man.

The ten sephiroth are also called the Ten Holy Emanations, and are divided into three columns or "pillars." (See Fig. 1.) The right-hand column is the Pillar of Mercy, to which is ascribed the male-active potency. The left-hand column is the Pillar of Judgment or Severity, to which is ascribed the female-passive principle. The Middle Pillar or Pillar of Mildness or Equilibrium is the harmonizing factor that blends and unites the Pillar of Mercy and the Pillar of Judgment.

From the preceding can be seen that the sephiroth on the right-hand column or Pillar of Mercy have masculine-positive qualities, while those on the left-hand column or Pillar of Judgment have feminine-negative properties. The sephiroth that form the Middle Pillar are transmitters or depositories of the other sephiroth, and as such have in them the seeds of both the male and the female potencies. Their essential quality is union, synthesis.

Each of the sephiroth is in a way androgynous or "bisexual" in essence, for it is feminine or receptive to

101

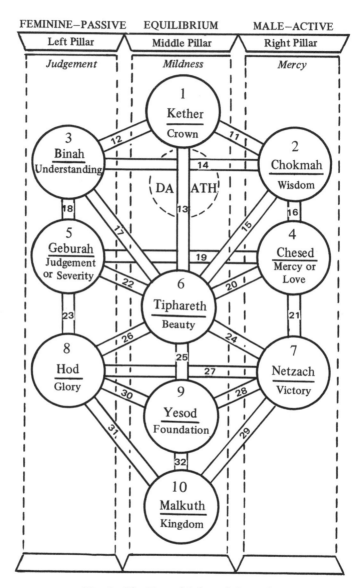

FEMININE–PASSIVE   EQUILIBRIUM   MALE–ACTIVE

Left Pillar   Middle Pillar   Right Pillar

Judgement   *Mildness*   *Mercy*

1
Kether
Crown

3
Binah
Understanding

DA ATH

2
Chokmah
Wisdom

5
Geburah
Judgement
or Severity

6
Tiphareth
Beauty

4
Chesed
Mercy or
Love

8
Hod
Glory

9
Yesod
Foundation

7
Netzach
Victory

10
Malkuth
Kingdom

Fig. 3   The Tree of Life and the Paths

the sephira that precedes it, and masculine or trans-missive to the sephira that follows it.

According to an ancient Kabbalistic tradition, the reason why the Deity placed the Pillar of Mildness or Middle Pillar between the Pillar of Mercy and the Pillar of Judgment was to control the outpouring of the positive or negative qualities of each sephira. An analogy may be given of a water faucet from which may flow hot or cold water. One may graduate the water temperature by simply turning the proper handle. When the necessary amount of water has been accumulated, another turn of the handle will halt the flow. The Middle Pillar may be likened to the handle of the water faucet, without which the water would flow uncontrollably, eventually causing a flood. The Pillar of Mercy has the quality of "limitless bestowal"; the Pillar of Judgment, on the other hand, is "unlimited restraint." Therefore if a man by virtue of a good action deserves Mercy, the Pillar of Mercy would bestow of its essence endlessly. However, since there is no man so perfect as to deserve such bounty, the Pillar of Judgment would come into action and neutralize and restrain the Pillar of Mercy. Therefore the Pillar of Mildness or Middle Pillar must act as a mediator to allow only that measure of Mercy that is necessary.

The three pillars of the Tree of Life are comparable to Ida, Shushumna, and Pingala of the Yoga system, where Shushumna is the channel of ascent of kundalini, placed between the male and female potencies of Ida and Pingala. The three pillars may be also likened to Yin and Yang, the female and male principles of Chinese philosophy, with Tao (the way) being analogous to the Middle Pillar. Modern Kabbalists, however, see the left and the right pillars as positive and negative phases of manifestation, while the Middle Pillar is seen as consciousness.*

As we have already stated, the Tree is seen as both the macrocosmus (the divine essence) and the microcosmus (man). When one looks at a diagram of the Tree, it is being observed as an objective symbol, and thus, as the macrocosmus. In order to see the Tree as the microcosmus, that is, as a blueprint of man's soul, one must "back into the Tree," so to speak, and project outwardly. The Tree then becomes a subjective symbol, for one is *in* it, the same as a figure in a photograph. When the Tree is seen as the microcosmus, the order of the columns is reversed, and the left-hand

* See Dion Fortune. *The Mystical Qabalah.* London, 1935.

Pillar becomes the right-hand Pillar and vice versa, the same as in a photographic negative.

The Ten Holy Emanations

Before the sephiroth were emanated, there was only the Infinite Light. According to the Kabbalah, before the present universe was created, "certain primordial worlds" were formed from the Light, but could not subsist as the Light had not yet been "restricted" and expressed as the female and male aspects of the Deity. These ancient pre-Creation worlds are the "kings of Edom," which are mentioned in the Bible. (Genesis 36:31)

As we have already seen, at the time of the restriction of the light, a point of light issued from the Infinite Source, forming the Archetypal Man, Adam Kadmon. This may be likened to a point within a circle. All the ten sephiroth were included in this point of light, or Primordial Point. As we know, although a point is imperceptible and undivisible, nevertheless it has three dimensions. If this were not so, we could not even conceive of it. The three dimensions are length, breadth, and depth. Each of these dimensions is also divided into three parts, beginning, middle, and end. We then have nine parts within this point, with the point itself making the number ten. The point and its nine dimensions are the ten sephiroth before emanation or manifestation was completed.

The three pillars are also encompassed in the Primordial Point, as follows:

1. Breadth—Pillar of Mercy
2. Depth—Pillar of Judgment
3. Length—Pillar of Mildness or Middle Pillar

It must be born in mind that when we speak of such terms as breadth, depth, length, beginning, middle, and end, we are referring to abstract concepts, as varying states of consciousness on different levels, that exist simultaneously in time and space.

From the Primordial Point the ten sephiroth were emanated in succession in the following order:

1. Kether—Crown:

This first sephira is the source of the other nine. To it is ascribed number 1, which encompasses within itself the other nine numbers of the decimal scale. Number 1 is the "monad" of the numerical symbolic ideas of Pythagoras. It is undivisible, but definable. And since definition projects an image or duplicate of the object defined, we find that by reflection of itself number 1 projects the other numbers. Thus it may be called the "father of all numbers" and a fitting image of the Father of all things.

Among the various titles given to Kether are Concealed of the Concealed, the Vast Countenance, the Primordial Point, the Point within a Circle, Macroprosopos, Ancient of Ancients. The Divine Name ascribed to this sphere is AHIH (Eheieh). Its archangel is Metraton. The angelical order, Chaioth ha Qadesh or Holy Living Creatures. Its correspondence in man is the cranium or skull.

Kether is outside human experience. Its essence cannot be comprehended by the human mind. In this sephira there is no form, but only "pure being" because in it there is no differentiation into a pair of opposites as yet.

The name of God ascribed to Kether is Eheieh, which means Existence. And that is what Kether is, the purest essence of existence, without any form or definition. In order to obtain an adequate concept of this formless state of latent existence, we may visualize it as void, formless, interstellar

107

space, which nevertheless harbors in it all the potentials of life.

Another title given to Kether is The First Swirlings. This implies the activity of the cosmic energy at the time of the creation of the universe. It is a fitting title because from the "first swirlings" sprang the second sephira, which is the first to be differentiated in one of the two modes of existence, male and female.

2. **Chokmah—Wisdom:**

To this sephira is ascribed the numeral 2. It is a masculine-active potency that is also known as Aba, the Father image, to whom the mother, the third sephira, is united.

Among the titles given to Chokmah are The Supernal Father, Power of Yetzirah, Yod of Tetragrammaton. The Divine Name of this sephira is Jehovah, the archangel is Ratziel, and the angelic order is the Auphanim, or Wheels. Its correspondence in man is the left side of the face. This sphere is identified with the Zodiac.

If we can compare Kether to a point, we can compare Chokmah to a line, which is an extension of the point into space. This straight line or "uplifted rod of power" may be equalized with the phallus, which is one of the esoteric symbols of this sephira. Chokmah is essentially dynamic, for within it is the seed of all creation. Its quality is Wisdom, which implies perfect knowledge and understanding. It is significant that the quality ascribed to the third sephira is understanding.

The phallus as a symbol of this sephira represents the dynamic, positive essence of Chokmah, for maleness is dynamism, just as femaleness is latency or potential force.

3. Binah—Understanding:

To this sephira is assigned the numeral 3. Binah is a feminine-passive potency, which is also called Ama, Mother, and Aima, the Fertile Mother, who is eternally "conjoined with Aba, the Father [Chokmah], for the maintenance of the universe in order." This sephira is also called Marah, the Great Sea, which is a root for Mary, and is known as the Mother of All Living. She is the supernal Mother, the feminine aspect of God, the Elohim. She is seen by Kabbalists as the archetypal womb through which all life comes into manifestation.

Some of the titles given to Binah are Ama, the dark, sterile mother, Aima, the bright, fertile mother, Khorsia, the Throne. The God name of this sephira is Jehovah Elohim, the archangel is Tzaphkiel, and the angelic order is the Aralim, or Thrones. Its correspondence in man is the right side of the face.

Whereas Chokmah is dynamic force, Binah is form, which is the container of force. The first letter of Binah is "Beth," which is the archetypal symbol of all containers.

In Binah and Chokmah we have two polarizing aspects of manifestations, the Supernal Father and Mother, from which the universe sprang. Together, Chokmah and Binah are the Elohim, the Creator Genesis speaks about. They are the two primordial blocks of life, proton and electron, that constitute all aspects of creation. In this first pair of sephiroth lies the key to sex, for they represent the biological opposites, male and female. These opposites, however, do not occur just in "space." They also occur in "time." We see them in the alternating periods in our lives, in the tides of the sea, in our physiological processes, and in international affairs. The alternating currents of activity and passivity, construction and destruction are the interplay of the two eternal opposites. It is interesting to note in this context that one of the symbols of Binah is the planet Saturn, also identified as Kronos, or Time. These cosmic tides are beautifully expressed in Shakespeare's words, "There is a tide in the affairs of men, which taken at the flood leads on to fortune."

While Wisdom is the quality of Chokmah, understanding is the essence of Binah. Wisdom suggests complete and infinite knowledge, while Understanding conveys the impression of the ability to grasp the concepts that are inherent in Wisdom. The Father knows all, but the Mother understands everything.

4. Chesed—Mercy:

To this sephira is ascribed the number 4. Chesed is a masculine potency, emanated from Binah as a result of her union with Chokmah. Chesed is also called Gedulah, which means Greatness or Magnificence. Its quality is Mercy or Love on a a higher, cosmic scale.

Among the titles given to Chesed are Gedulah and Majesty. The God name is El, the archangel is Tzadkiel, and the angelic order is the Chasmalim or Brilliant Ones. Its correspondence in man is the left arm, and it is also identified with the planet Jupiter.

Chesed is the first sephira that may be conceived by the human mind, for it is the concretion of the abstract concepts formulated by the three Supernals, Kether, Chokmah, and Binah.

Whereas Chokmah may be likened to the All-Knowing Father, the "All-Begetter," Chesed is the loving, protecting father, forgiving and generous.

Betwen the three supernals and the other seven sephiroth there is a chasm, which is known by Kabbalists as the Abyss. This pit is a demarcation of varying degrees of consciousness. The three supernals symbolize those higher states of consciousness that transcend human awareness. The lower sephiroth function within the realm of ideas and as such are the only ones we can apprehend with our normal consciousness. In order to grasp the abstract essence of the higher sephiroth, we have to cross the gulf of the Abyss, which implies leaving the confinement of our personalities, to reach our Higher Self, the great unconscious.

5. **Geburah—Strength, Severity:**

To this sephira is ascribed the numeral 5. Geburah is a feminine potency, emanated from Chesed.

The titles given to this sephira are Din, Justice, and Pachad, Fear. The God name is Elohim Gebor, the archangel is Khamael, and the angelic order is the Seraphim or Fiery Serpents. Its correspondence in man is the right arm. It is identified with the planet Mars.

Geburah is the most forceful and disciplined of the sephiroth. Its force is not an evil force unless its essence overflows from justice into cruelty. This is the symbolism of Mars, which is also the Roman god of war and strife. To Kabbalists, Geburah is essentially a conciliatory force, a restriction of the merciful love of Chesed. Without the strong arm of Geburah the mercies of Chesed would degenerate into folly and cowardice.

Geburah may be likened to fire, which may be used constructively or destructively. Its power for destruction may be curtailed by careful control of the flame. In Geburah we find the element of awe, the "fear of God," which, according to the Scriptures, is necessary for salvation.

6. Tiphareth—Beauty:

To this sephira is ascribed the number 6. Its position is in the middle of the Tree of Life, in the Pillar of Mildness or Equilibrium. It is an emanation of Chesed and Geburah.

The titles given to Tiphareth are Zoar Anpin, the Lesser Countenance; Melekh, the King; Adam; the Son; and the Man. The God name is Jehovah Aloah Va Daath, the archangel is Raphael, and the angelic order is the Malachim or Kings. Its correspondence in man is the breast. It is also identified with the sun.

In Tiphareth we see that by the union of Mercy and Justice (Chesed and Geburah) we obtain Beauty or Clemency, which completes the second triad of the Tree of Life.

Tiphareth is the center of equilibrium of the Tree of Life. As such it is seen as a link, a point of transition. The four sephiroth represent the Higher self, while Kether is the Divine spark in which is the seed of manifestation. The four lower sephiroth are representative of the personality or lower self.

Two of the symbols ascribed to Tiphareth are a child and a sacrificed god, in which may be seen both the Christ and the Egyptian god, Osiris. In

114

the child we see a beginning that ends in the sacrificed god for the purpose of transformation of the material into the Divine. This aspect of Tiphareth is "the point of transmutation between the planes of force and the planes of form."

Another symbol of this sephira is the sun, the giver of life, which may also be found in the gold of the alchemists.

7. Netzach—Victory:

The numeral ascribed to this sephira is 7. Netzach is a male potency, emanated from Tiphareth.

The title given to Netzach is Firmness. The God name is Jehovah Tzabaoth, the archangel is Haniel, and the angelic order is the Elohim or gods. Its correspondence in man is the hips and legs.

It is identified with the planet Venus.

Netzach represents the instincts and the emotions. It is a sphere densely populated with the thought forms of the group mind. Thus it is essentially an illusory plane, where the archetypal ideas have not yet been expressed as forms.

The planet Venus, which is ascribed to Netzach, is also a symbol of the Roman goddess of love. Venus is not a fertility goddess like Ceres or Persephone. She is pure emotion. And the essence of this emotion is never crystallized into form. This may be seen clearly from the fact that the hips and legs which are assigned to this sephira are the seat of the generative organs, but not the generative organs themselves. Netzach, then, represents the instinctive, emotional side of our nature.

8. **Hod—Glory:**

To this sephira is assigned the number 8. Hod is a feminine potency, emanated from Netzach. The God name of this sephira is Elohim Tzabaoth, the archangel is Michael, and the angelic order is the Ben Elohim or Sons of God. Its correspondence in man is the loins and the legs. It is identified with the planet Mercury.

Hod is the seat of the intellectual powers in man. It is the sphere where the emotions and instincts of Netzach finally take form and come into action. Hod and Netzach must always function together, for just as the instinct or emotion cannot be manifested without the creative power of the intellect, the intellect cannot manifest itself without the thought forms that arise out of instinct and emotion.

In the Practical Kabbalah, Hod is the sphere of

magic because it is the sephira where forms are created. The practicing Kabbalist uses this sephira to formulate with his mind images of things he wants to attain in the material plane. Since Hod is the seat of the intellect or human mind, any thought forms projected from Netzach into it may be impressed upon the higher consciousness, which will then bring the images thus formed into realization.

9. Yesod—Foundation:

The number ascribed to this sephira is 9. It is located in the Middle Pillar and is a result of the union between Netzach and Hod. The God name of Yesod is Shaddai El Chai, the Almighty Living God. The archangel is Gabriel and the angelic order is the Kerubim or the Strong. Its correspondence is the reproductive organs. It is identified with the Moon.

Yesod is the seat of intuition in man. It is the sphere of the Astral Light and the receptacle of the emanations of the other sephiroth. According to the Kabbalah the function of Yesod is to purify and "correct" the emanations. Yesod, which is essentially the sphere of the moon, reflects the light of Tiphareth, which is the sphere of the sun. Therefore the light of Yesod-Moon is always in a state of flux and reflux because the amount of sunlight received waxes and wanes in a twenty-eight-day cycle.

Since Yesod is the sphere of the moon, it is ruled by the moon goddess, which is seen in her various aspects of Diana, the virgin goddess of the Greeks; Isis, the fertile moon goddess of the Egyptians; and Hecate, the goddess of witchcraft and of childbirth. The reason why the mystical moon is sometimes seen as a virgin and other times as a fertile mother may be found in the rhythmical nature of the moon and of the sex life of the female. The magnetism of all living creatures is affected by these lunar tides. To Yesod is also assigned the element of water. The lunar tides also affect the oceans and the body fluids in man. The magnetic influence of the moon can only operate through the sphere of Yesod.

10. Malkuth—Kingdom:

To this sephira is ascribed the number 10. Malkuth is an emanation of Yesod and represents the material world. It is also known as the Queen, the Inferior Mother, the Bride of Macroprosopos and the Shekinah. It is the last of the sephiroth and it is placed in the Middle Pillar.

Some of the titles given to Malkuth are the Gate of Death, the Gate of the Garden of Eden, the Virgin. The God name is Adonai Ha Aretz, the Archangel is Sandalphon, and the angelic order is the Ashim or Souls of Fire. Its correspondence in man is the feet and the anus. It is also identified with the planet earth and with the four elements.

Malkuth is essentially the sphere of man, of sensation. It is also the only sephira that does not form part of a triad. It is therefore seen by the Kabbalists as a container for the emanations of the other nine sephiroth.

Malkuth is the seat of matter and also of fire, water, air, and earth, the four elements of the ancients. The physicist recognizes three states of matter—solid, liquid, and gas. These three modes of matter correspond to the elements of earth, air, and water, while electricity corresponds to the element of fire. The esotericist classifies all physical phenomena under these four elements in order to understand their nature.

The intrinsic quality of Malkuth is stability, the inertia of matter that is like the sway of a pendulum rhythmically oscillating throughout eternity.

The Zohar describes the Infinite Light as a

very expansive sea, for the waters of the sea are themselves without limit or form. It is only when they spread themselves upon the earth that they assume a form. Following is the order of the development of the sephiroth: the source of the sea's water and the water stream that comes therefrom are the first two sephiroth, Crown and Wisdom; a great reservoir is then formed just as if a huge hollow had been dug, and this is called a sea. It is the sephira Understanding, which is called Marah, the Great Sea. This reservoir is an unfathomable deep which issues seven streams, which are the seven channels or sephiroth: Mercy, Judgment, Beauty, Victory, Glory, Foundation, and Kingdom. The source, the water stream, the sea, and the seven streams make up the ten sephiroth.

The ten sephiroth are classified in five stages or phases, which are known as "worlds.'" In the beginning, the first ten sephiroth that emanated from the Infinite Light were too powerful and man could not receive illumination from them. It was then necessary

120

for these initial sephiroth to be extended further, veiling their light so that man could receive it. The process had to be repeated four times until the light was sufficiently diffuse for man to partake of the Infinite Light. This resulted in the Four Worlds of the Kabbalists, which we have already discussed. The first world that emanated from the Infinite Light in the form of the Primordial Point was that of Adam Kadmon. The next world that emanated from Adam Kadmon was the World of Emanation of Atziluth, also composed of ten sephiroth, but with dimmer lights. Then came the ten sephiroth that made the World of Creation, or Briah, followed by the World of Formation, Yetzirah, and lastly, the World of Action, Assiah, which is also the world of man.

The distance in degree between the worlds of the sephiroth is carefully stipulated according to Divine decree, by which this order was arranged for the purpose of creation. It is interesting to note that the famous Bode-Titius rule of planetary distances states that within our planetary system, the "distance of each world from the sun is approximately twice the distance of the previous one," almost as if it had been stipulated according to Divine decree.

In each of the five worlds, the World of Adam Kadmon and the Four Kabbalistic Worlds, the ten sephiroth are divided into three triads, composed of the first nine sephiroth, and the last sephira, Malkuth.

The first triad is formed by the three "Supernals," Kether, Chokmah, and Binah. The Kabbalistic books give many "strange" names to the sephiroth, but each of these titles has a distinct reason for being, for they are in fact precise metaphysical terms of almost scientific accuracy. The actual meaning of Kether in the Hebrew language is Crown. Chokmah means Wisdom and Binah means Understanding. A "crown" is a kingly attribute that is placed on top of the head. The "magical" image associated with Kether is that of a Bearded King seen in profile. This sephira is also known as The Head Which Is Not. In all this symbolism we see distinct correspondences with the human head, which in the world of archetypal ideas represents the highest level of consciousness. Indeed, The Head Which Is Not is a clear image of a superconsciousness that lies outside the realm of human experience and thus cannot be encompassed within the limits of the human brain. It is the Crown that adorns the brow of the Bearded King seen in profile, which is none other than Adam Kadmon, the first manifestation of the Divine Light.

The first outpouring from the Crown, which is Kether, is Wisdom, the absolute, perfect knolwedge that is an attribute of this higher consciousness. Chokmah, which is Wisdom, is also the Supernal Father.

From Wisdom springs forth Understanding, which is Binah, the Supernal Mother, the Great Sea. From this symbolism we conceive the idea of the vast waters of interstellar space where worlds were created. We are also reminded that the first manifestation of primordial life, in the form of the first unicellular organism, arose from the waters.

Binah is also known as Ama, the Dark Sterile Mother, and as Aima, the Bright Fertile Mother. As we have already stated, she is also Marah, the Great Sea. Marah is the root of Mary. Thus we have a concept of a virgin (Ama) which becomes a mother (Aima) by the power of the Holy Spirit.

The secret of the transition of Binah from the Dark Sterile Mother (Ama) to the Bright Fertile Mother (Aima) is in another sephira that lies concealed midway between the sphere of Chokmah and that of Binah. This "hidden" sephira is called Daath, and its meaning is Knowledge. When we refer to the Bible and find that sexual encounters between a man and a woman are described as a man *knowing* a woman, we

have a clear "Understanding" of the properties of
Daath. An example of this is found in Genesis 4:1,
"And Adam knew Eve his wife; and she conceived,
and bare Cain, and said, I have gotten a man from the
Lord." The position of Daath between the two spheres
of Chokmah and Binah, the Supernal Father and the
Supernal Mother, makes it obvious that the Kabbalistic "secret" of their union is sex. This Knowledge that
is Daath, conceived in the material plane as the sexual
union between a male and a female, is what made
possible the transition of Binah from virgin (Dark
Sterile Mother) to mother (Bright Fertile Mother).

In the archetypal world to which the three Supernals belong, the concept of Daath is not one of sex in
the physical sense of the word, but of realization and
illumination. It is the union of cosmic opposites for
the purpose of manifestation. In the words of modern
Kabbalist Dion Fortune. "Daath is the secret of both
generation and regeneration, the key to the manifestation of all things through the differentation into
pairs of Opposites and their union in a Third." In the
Supernal Triad, Kether, Chokmah, and Binah, we
have the key to our cosmogony.

The second Triad is formed by the fourth, fifth, and
sixth sephiroth: Chesed (Mercy), Geburah (Judg-

ment), and Tiphareth (Beauty). The union between the Supernal Mother and the Supernal Father by means of Daath gave birth to Mercy, which is also called Love. Thus we see how on the archetypal planes the union of the male and female principles gives rise to that which on the material plane is the most sublime feeling man can experience. Mercy emanates Judgment, which is also known as Strength. Chesed or Mercy is, as we have seen, also a Father image, while Geburah is a Mother image, strong and severe. From this "Strong Love" that is the union of Chesed and Geburah is born Tiphareth or Beauty, the sixth sephira, which is also known as The Son, and has the image of a child as one of its symbols. Tiphareth is situated in the Middle Pillar, directly underneath the sphere of Daath. We see therefore how through the realization that is Daath, the Supernal Mother, Binah, "gave birth" to Chesed, Mercy or Love, which then united with Geburah, Strength, to "give birth" to Tiphareth, The Son. This triad symbolizes the evolution of ideas conceived in the archetypal matrix of the Three Supernals.

The third triad is composed of the seventh, eighth, and ninth sephiroth: Netzach (Victory), Hod (Glory), and Yesod (Foundation). Netzach is a male potency that reflects the pure love of Mercy on a lower plane, that of emotions and instincts. Thus the Divine love that was emitted from Binah into Chesed becomes sexual desire in Netzach. The emotions that are the essence of this sephira have not yet been manifested into action; they may be likened to the instinctual drives in man, before they are channeled into form. In Netzach we find all the basic instincts and emotions latent in man, from the instinct of preservation to ambition and raw passion. But before these tenuous thought forms may find expression, Netzach must emanate and then fuse with Hod (Glory), which is the seat of intellectual endeavor and the will of man. The union of the will of Hod and the emotions of Netzach give rise to the next sephira, Yesod, which is represented by the sexual organs in man. Through Hod, therefore, the sexual desires latent in Netzach find actual expression and form in a physical vehicle. They are then "realized." And since Yesod is also placed in the Middle Pillar, the same as Daath, we see how the sephira of Foundation is really the realization of Daath on a lower plane. But Yesod is also seen as the sphere of the Moon and of intuition. Therefore it is still not realization on a physical plane, but on a mental level. This triad is seen by Kabbalists, as the Astral World, where all forms are composed of a plastic, etheric substance, which acts like a matrix to the physical world. All the actions that take place in the material world must first be "shaped" and actualized in the Astral World. This is the action of the union of Hod and Netzach.

Below the third and last triad is the lone sphere of Malkuth, which represents the material world. The restriction of the Infinite Light being completed, the nether world of form and action comes into manifestation. Here is the seat of the four elements of the alchemists—fire, water, air, and earth—which must not be conceived as their material counterparts, but rather as cosmic essence brought into differentiation. It was to the "qualities" of the elements that the ancients referred and not to the elements themselves. Thus we see in the element of fire the quality of expansion, and also of heat, which is evident in the material world in the physical phenomena of combustion, digestion, and oxidation. The quality of the element of water is contraction, which is seen in muscular action and in the solidification of water into ice. The quality of the element of air is locomotion, mova-

Fig. 4   Kabbalistic Square

The square connotes the four sides of the world. The upper side is "East," the lower side is "West," the right side is "South" and the left side is "North." The four diagonal lines are another square that links all the corners of the world and causes the admixture of the diverse climates to each side of the world. These are the four basic elements: Air is East, earth is West, fire is South and water is North. Warmth and dryness is the nature of the fire element. Moisture and coldness is the nature of the water element. Because the East and West sides are connected with the South and North sides, it follows that East and West partake of a double climate due to being linked to the South and the North sides of the world. East, which is air, has the warmth of the South and moisture of the North, therefore its climate is warm and moist. The warmth is derived from the fire element of the South and its moisture from the water element of the North. The West side, which is earth, gets its dryness from the fire—South, and its coldness from the water —North. Therefore, the nature of the earth is cold and dry.

128

Fig. 5   The Star of David

bility, which does not need to be exemplified. And lastly, the quality of the element of earth is inertia, cohesion, which are qualities of solid matter.

The qualities of expansion, concentration, locomotion, or movement and cohesion (union) are all external manifestations of the World of Action, Malkuth. They can be seen not just in physical phenomena but also in human relations and in international affairs. The interplay of the forces of expansion and contraction (fire and water) can be seen in the two triangles that form the Star of David. The upward-pointing triangle symbolizes fire, while the downward-pointing triangle represents water. Tradition teaches that King David was a master Kabbalist, and this symbol is strongly indicative that indeed he was. For by means of the proper interaction of strength

(Fire) and restraint (Water), so visually expressed in the Star of David, he was able to unify Israel after generations of strife and dissolution.

In Malkuth, then, we see the materialization of the intangible and abstract concepts that originate in the higher spheres. It is in this last sephira, also known as Kingdom, that the Bearded King of Kether reigns in all His Glory. It was to this Kingdom (Malkuth) that Jesus referred in the last part of the Lord's Prayer (Matthew 6:13), "For thine is the Kingdom (Malkuth), and the Power (Netzach), and the Glory (Hod), forever. Amen." It is obvious that only a consummate Kabbalist could have composed this prayer.

The ten sephiroth are also divided by Kabbalists into Arik Anpin (the Vast Countenance), Zaur Anpin (the Lesser Countenance), and the Bride of Microprosopos. Arik Anpin, which is also known as Macroprosopos, is formed by the Three Supernals, Kether, Chokmah, and Binah. Zaur Anpin, or Microprosopos, is composed of Chesed, Geburah, Tiphareth, Netzach, Hod, and Yesod. The Bride of Microprosopos is the sephira Malkuth, which is sometimes referred to as the Queen, or the Inferior Mother. Microprosopos is called also Melech, or the King.

TABLE 3

The Divine Names and the Tree of Life

Sephira	God Name	Archangel	Order of Angels
1. Kether	Eheieh	Metatron	Chaioth ha Qadesh
2. Chokmah	Jehovah	Ratziel	Auphanim
3. Binah	Jehovah Elohim	Tzaphkiel	Aralim
4. Chesed	El	Tzadkiel	Chasmalim
5. Geburah	Elohim Gebor	Khamael	Seraphim
6. Tiphareth	Jehovah Aloah va Daath	Raphael	Malachim
7. Netzach	Jehovah Tzabaoth	Haniel	Elohim
8. Hod	Elohim Tzabaoth	Michael	Beni Elohim
9. Yesod	Shaddai el Chai	Gabriel	Kerubim
10. Malkuth	Adonai Ha Aretz	Sandalphon	Ashim

The Tree of Life in the Four Worlds

As we have already discussed, the ten sephiroth that
form the Tree of Life were emanated from the Infinite Light into the Primordial World of Adam Kadmon
and thence to the Four Worlds of the Kabbalists. The
sephira Kingdom (Malkuth), which is the densest of
the sephiroth, and in which the Divine Light is more
restricted, is the source for each of the next worlds.
Thus we see that the sephira Kingdom of Adam Kadmon emanated the ten sephiroth of the World of
Emanation, and the sephira Kingdom of the World
of Emanation issued the ten sephiroth of the World of
Creation, and so on, until the world of Action was
emanated. In the World of Emanation God acts directly, in the World of Creation He acts through the
archangels, in the World of Formation He acts
through the angels, and in the World of Action He
acts through the elemental forces of Nature.

The Four Worlds, therefore, form a vast system of
classification that expresses all the aspects of the
Cosmic Essence at any level. (See Table 3.)

The most important divisions that are classified
within the Four Worlds are the four elements of the
alchemists, the four seasons, and the four astrological

triplicities. There is also a color scale (see Table 4) assigned to each sephira in each of the Four Worlds, which is of great significance in the practical Kabbalah. Each of the worlds falls under the supervision of one of the letters of the Tetragrammaton, IHVH, as follows: The first letter, I, is the World of Emanation; the second letter, H, is the World of Creation; V stands for the World of Formation; and the last letter, H, is the World of Action.

The Tetragrammaton, also known as Jehovah, is the God name assigned to the second sephira, Chokmah. The first sephira, Kether, is under the presidency of another four-letter name: Eheieh (AHIH). Through the symbolism of the names we see how AHIH, which is that aspect of God that is latent force, as yet unmanifested, transmutes Itself into IHVH by changing Its first and third letters from A (Aleph) to I (Yod) and from I (Yod) to V (Vau). As we have seen in the analysis of the twenty-two letters of the Hebrew alphabet, Aleph is the dual principle that represents life and death, existence; and indeed, existence is the meaning of the name AHIH. Yod, on the other hand, is the opposite of Aleph; it is continuity, the manifestation of existence. Thus in the first transmutation, the Cosmic Energy is transformed from

133

pure existence into continuous existence, steady-state. The second transmutation involves the exchange of a Yod (I) to a Vau (V). As we have seen, Vau is the archetype of all fertilizing substances, it is the plastic substance whence the universe sprang. Through this transmutation, AHIH, pure being, is transformed into IHVH, which is the vehicle of existence. In this transformation lies the essence of the Kabbalistic teaching.

Tetragrammaton, then, is the continuous (I) pulsation of cosmic energy (H) evolving (V) into the created universe (H). According to astrophysics, these were the conditions existing at the time of the "big-bang theory."

The Tetragrammaton and the Four Worlds are also associated with the four kerubim of Ezekiel's vision and the biblical revelation of St. John the Divine. Again, there is a correlation with the four elements and the astrological triplicities, as follows:

Letter	Kerubim	Element	Zodiacal Sign	World
I	Man Image	Air	Aquarius	Emanation
H	Lion	Fire	Leo	Creation
V	Eagle	Water	Scorpio	Formation
H	Bull	Earth	Taurus	Action

From the preceding we see that in order to know the qualities of any of the sephiroth of the Tree of Life, it is necessary to know its correspondences in all the Four Worlds. This is no mean task when we consider the vastness of the classification system that is the Kabbalah.

The Paths

According to the Sepher Yetzirah there are thirty-two Paths of Wisdom, but in reality, there are only twenty-two paths. The other ten are ascribed to the ten sephiroth for reasons best known to the ancient Kabbalists.

The twenty-two Paths correspond to the twenty-two letters of the Hebrew alphabet, but according to the Practical Kabbalah they are also assigned to the twelve signs of the Zodiac, the seven planets, and the four elements. The element of earth, however, is usually assigned to the sephira Malkuth, so that the remaining twenty-two symbols correspond exactly to the twenty-two Paths. These subtle discrepancies in Kabbalistic symbolism are seen by many as intended

"blinds" designed by the ancient Kabbalists to mis-
guide the profane.

As we have already seen, the Paths are connecting
lines betwen the various sephiroth. The best description of the Paths, in the opinion of this writer, is that
of Johannes Stephanus Rittangelius (1642), translated
from its original Hebrew by W. Wynn Westcott. We
can do no better than cite it here. We will omit the
first ten paths, since, as we have stated, they are assigned to the ten sephiroth. Following, then, are the
descriptions of the twenty-two Paths, from eleven to
thirty-two, according to Rittangelius:

11th Path—(connecting Kether and Chokmah)
> "The Eleventh Path is the Scintillating Intelli-
> gence, because it is the essence of that curtain
> which is placed close to the order of the dispo-
> sition, and this is a special dignity given to it
> that it may be able to stand before the Face of
> the Cause of Causes."

12th Path—(connecting Kether and Binah)
> "The Twelfth Path is the Intelligence of Trans-
> parency because it is that species of Magnifi-
> cence called *Chazchazit* (vision), which is
> named the place whence issues the vision of

those seeing in apparitions. (That is, the pro-
phecies by seers in a vision.)"

13th Path—(connecting Kether and Tiphareth)

"The Thirteenth Path is named the Uniting Intelligence, and is so called because it is itself
the Essence of Glory. It is the consummation of
the Truth of individual spiritual things."

14th Path—(connecting Binah and Chokmah)

"The Fourteenth Path is the Illuminating Intelligence, and is so called because it is that
Chasmal (scintillating flame) which is the
founder of the concealed and fundamental
ideas of holiness and of their stages of preparation."

15th Path—(connecting Chokmah and Tiphareth)

"The Fifteenth Path is the Constituting Intelligence, so called because it constitutes the
substance of creation in pure darkness, and
men have spoken of these contemplations; it is
that darkness spoken of in Scripture, Job 38:9,
'and thick darkness a swaddling band for it.'"

16th Path—(connecting Chokmah and Chesed)

"The Sixteenth Path is the Triumphal or Eternal Intelligence, so called because it is the
pleasure of the Glory, beyond which is no

Glory like to it, and it is called also the Paradise prepared for the Righteous."

17th Path—(connecting Binah and Tiphareth)

"The Seventeenth Path is the Disposing Intelligence, which provides faith to the righteous, and they are clothed with the Holy Spirit by it, and it is called the Foundation of Excellence in the state of higher things."

18th Path—(connecting Binah and Geburah)

"The Eighteenth Path is called the House of Influence (by the greatness of whose abundance the influx of good things upon created beings is increased), and from the midst of the investigation the arcana and hidden senses are drawn forth, which dwell in its shade and which cling to it, from the cause of all causes."

19th Path—(connecting Chesed and Geburah)

"The Nineteenth Path is the Intelligence of all the activities of the spiritual beings, and is so called because of the affluence diffused by it from the most high blessing and most exalted sublime glory."

20th Path—(connecting Chesed and Tiphareth)

"The Twentieth Path is the Intelligence of Will, and is so called because it is the means of preparation of all and each created being, and by this intelligence the existence of the Primordial Wisdom becomes known."

21st Path—(connecting Chesed and Netzach)

"The Twenty-first Path is the Intelligence of Conciliation, and is so called because it receives the divine influence which flows into it from its benediction upon all and each existence."

22nd Path—(connecting Geburah and Tiphareth)

"The Twenty-second Path is the Faithful Intelligence and is so called because by it spiritual virtues are increased, and all dwellers on earth are nearly under its shadow."

23rd Path—(connecting Geburah and Hod)

"The Twenty-third Path is the Stable Intelligence, and it is so called because it has the virtue of consistency among all numerations."

24th Path—(connecting Tiphareth and Netzach)

"The Twenty-fourth Path is the Imaginative Intelligence and it is so called because it gives a likeness to all the similitudes which are created in like manner similar to its harmonius elegancies."

25th Path—(connecting Tiphareth and Yesod)

"The Twenty-fifth Path is the Intelligence of Probation, or is Tentative, and is so called because it is the primary temptation, by which the Creator trieth all righteous persons."

26th Path—(connecting Tiphareth and Hod)

"The Twenty-sixth Path is called the Renovating Intelligence because the Holy God renews it by all the changing things which are renewed by the creation of the world."

27th Path—(connecting Netzach and Hod)

"The Twenty-seventh Path is the Exciting Intelligence and it is so called because through it is consummated the nature of every existent being under the orb of the Sun, in perfection."

28th Path—(connecting Netzach and Yesod)

The Twenty-eighth Path is not described in this translation.

29th Path—(connecting Netzach and Malkuth)

"The Twenty-ninth Path is the Corporeal Intelligence, so called because it forms every body which is formed beneath the whole set of worlds and the increment of them."

30th Path—(connecting Hod and Yesod)

"The Thirtieth Path is the Collecting Intelligence, and is so called because Astrologers deduce from it the judgement of the stars, and of the celestial signs, and the perfections of their science, according to the rules of their resolutions."

31st Path—(connecting Hod and Malkuth)

"The Thirty-first Path is the Perpetual Intelligence: but why is it so called? Because it regulates the motions of the Sun and Moon in their proper order, each in an orbit convenient for it."

32nd Path—(connecting Yesod and Malkuth)

"The Thirty-second Path is the Administrative Intelligence and it is so called because it directs and associates in all their operations the seven planets, even all of them in their own due course."

The Qliphoth

According to Kabbalistic tradition, when the cosmic energy was overflowing from Kether (the first sephira) to form Chokmah, its force was not fully stabilized, for it still lacked form and direction. From this surplus of excess energy, the adverse sephiroth or Qliphoth were evolved. (Qliphah is the singular

141

form of the noun, and it means a woman of easy virtue, a harlot.)

The Qliphoth, then, are a group of ten sephiroth, unbalanced and chaotic, that are the complete opposites of the harmonious forces that form the Tree of Life. As such, they are termed evil, and are the infernal regions mentioned in the Bible. They are not independent principles in the cosmic scale, but the "unbalanced and destructive aspects" of the spheres of the Tree of Life. Therefore, there are two Trees, and they both must be taken into consideration for the proper understanding of the Kabbalistic doctrine. For wherever there is a virtue or positive sephira, there is a corresponding vice, which is symbolized by the adverse Qliphah.

The two Trees, Sephirotic and Qliphotic, are often represented as if the infernal spheres, which are on the reverse side of the Divine ones, like the opposite side of a coin, were a reflection of the Tree of Life, from a mirror placed at its base. In this concept, the Qliphoth seem to extend downward from the sphere of Malkuth, where they abut. Malkuth, according to tradition, is a "fallen sephira," for it was separated from the rest of the Tree by Adam's Fall. Thus the material world rests upon the top of the infernal

142

world of "shells.' That is the reason why their influence is felt so strongly in human affairs.

The demons of the Qliphoth are the most unbalanced and chaotic of all principles. The first two spheres of the Qliphotic Tree, corresponding inversely to Kether and Chockmah, are void and disorganized, while the third sphere is known as "the abode of darkness." The reigning prince of the Qliphoth is Samael, "the angel of poison and death." He corresponds to the sphere of Crown, Kether, and also answers by the name of Satan. His wife, Isheh Zenunim, is the harlot, and corresponds to the sphere of Chokmah. From their union springs the Beast, Chiva, often represented by Satanists as a goat with female breasts. Together, they form the infernal trinity in direct opposition to the Three Supernals. Below the first demonic triad are the seven hells, which are occupied by cohorts of devils who represent all the vices and crimes of humanity, and whose infernal duties are to torture and inflict punishment on those who abandon themselves to those vices.

The pentagram, or five-pointed star, is one of the symbols used to indicate the harmonious (Sephiroth) or chaotic (Qliphoth) forces of the Cosmos. The five points of the pentagram symbolize the four elements

143

Fig. 6   The Pentagrams

of the ancients, plus a fifth element, which is known as "akasha" or ether. This fifth element is not to be confused with the material concept of ether. It is a every tenuous "substance" which is found only in the abstract worlds. Just as the four elements are assigned to the Four Worlds of the Kabbalists, this fifth element is ascribed to the archetypal world of Adam Kadmon. When the pentagram is used to symbolize the harmonizing forces of the elements in the Tree of Life, the glyph is presented with one point uppermost and two points extending on either side, like a man standing with open arms, absorbing into his soul the

144

bounties of the Divine Light. The two lower points represent the figure's spread legs. The Tetragrammation, or IHVH, is also hidden in the pentagram, as follows: the upper point of the Yod (I) corresponds to the upper point of the pentagram, or the World of Adam Kadmon; the body of the Yod corresponds to the right point of the star and the World of Emanation; the letter He (H) corresponds to the right-hand "leg" of the pentagram and to the World of Creation; the letter Vau (V) corresponds to the left-hand "leg" and to the World of Formation, while the last letter He (H) corresponds to the left point of the pentagram and to the World of Action.

When the position of the pentagram is reversed, the two lower points, which form the "legs" of the glyph, are placed uppermost. The pentagram then resembles the head of a goat, where the two points form the horns, the points protruding on the sides are the ears and the lower point forms a beard. This is a common symbol among Satanists, by means of which they contact the adverse Qliphoth, the infernal habitations of the demonic hordes.

From the preceding discussion we see that the Qliphoth are the result of the unbalanced surplus of energy that gave rise to the sephiroth of the Tree of

Life. This unbalanced force forms the center around which revolve all the evil thought forms of mankind. It is therefore the source as well as the consequence of all man's evil thoughts and actions. Because the Qliphoth were evolved from an overflow of cosmic energy, their influence is directly related to excess in any form. Thus, an excess of love gives rise to jealousy, an excess in sexual desire gives rise to lust, an excess of worldly ambition leads to avarice, until all the gamut of human qualities and inspirations are debased and vilified.

The infernal Qliphoth is seen by Kabbalists as the monster Leviathan, the serpent that rears its ugly head behind the shoulders of the Bride of Micropro-sopos, the Queen, Malkuth, also known as the World of Men.

The Practical Kabbalah

It is not the purpose of this book to go into the practical aspects of the Kabbalah, with its array of rituals and magical ceremonies. Such a task would necessitate a whole book to elucidate the intricacies of the magical realms of the Kabbalah. Therefore we will confine ourselves to a general discussion of the magi-

146

cal aspects of the Kabbalistic doctrine, and how they are applied by the Kabbalists in order to achieve results on the material planes.

Something must be said at this juncture about the "ascent" or "descent" of power through the various spheres of the Tree of Life. As we have already seen, the Tree of Life is the essence of the Kabbalah. It is also the working tool of the practicing Kabbalist. To elucidate this point further, let us look into the two methods that are used by the Kabbalists to "draw power" from the Tree.

The first method that we will discuss is used only by mystics, or by those who wish to acquire illumination, or, which is the same thing, to establish a perfect equilibrium within their personalities and a total harmony with the soul of the universe. This method is known as "the Path of the Arrow, which is shot from the Bow of Promise, Quesheth, the rainbow of astral colors that spreads like a halo behind Yesod."* This system does not confer any magical powers, and is used by the mystic to·rise from the material world to the higher planes of exalted consciousness. It is called the Path of the Arrow because it moves in

* See Dion Fortune. *The Mystical Qabalah*. London, 1935.

a straight line from Malkuth, through Yesod and Tip-hareth, traversing Daath and the Abyss, directly into Kether. The process is conducted chiefly through meditation upon the various symbols associated with the sephiroth just mentioned, which are all placed upon the Middle Pillar. There are no worldly ambitions in the hearts of the mystics who follow this Path, only the desire to unite with their Higher Selves and to blend with the soul of Nature. The rewards of this Path are, as we have said, illumination, and the perfect equilibrium of the personality.

The second method is used by practicing Kabbalists as a magical system. It is known as the Flash of Lightning, and it is also likened to the coils of a serpent that extend in zig zag throughout the tree, traversing its whole length, sephira by sephira. Contrary to the Path of the Arrow, which is an ascending Path, the Flash of Lightning is mostly for the "descent of power." In order to bring down power the practicing Kabbalist, or magician, must have a perfect knowledge of the Tree of Life and of the correspondences of the various sephiroth. This means he must know the God name assigned to each sephira, as well as the archangels and the angelic orders. He must also be familiar with the various color scales of the Tree, as each of the Four Kabbalistic Worlds has a color scheme assigned to it. For the purpose of magical work, the color scale used is that of the World of Creation, which is known as the "Queen Scale" (see Table 4). The practicing Kabbalist must also know by heart the various magical images and the symbols ascribed to each sephira, because it is by means of these images and symbols that he will attempt to contact the forces represented by the spheres of the Tree. Once he is equipped with this formidable array of magical symbolism, the Kabbalist proceeds to invoke the force that he wants to contact in the tree (see Table 5). The forces in the tree are elemental in nature, they may be likened to a plastic substance with which one can shape and mold different forms. It is the etheric substance known as the akasha. Once the Kabbalist has contacted the sphere he is working with, he proceeds to mold, by means of powerful visualization, the images of the things he wishes to acquire in the material plane. When he has finished doing this, he brings down the force from its place in the Tree to his material level. This last part is the most difficult to accomplish, and is known by occultists as "earthing" the force. If the magician fails to "earth" the force he has contacted, the purpose of the cere-

149

150

TABLE 4   The Color Scales and
the Tree of Life in the Four Worlds

Sephiroth	Atziluth (King Scale)	Briah* (Queen Scale)	Yetzirah (Emperor Scale)	Assiah (Empress Scale)
1. Kether	Brilliance	White brilliance	White brilliance	White, flecked gold
2. Chokmah	Light blue	Gray	Iridescent gray	White, flecked with red, blue, yellow
3. Binah	Crimson	Black	Dark brown	Gray, flecked with pink
4. Chesed	Violet	Blue	Purple	Azure, flecked with yellow
5. Geburah	Orange	Red	Scarlet	Red, flecked with black
6. Tiphareth	Rose pink	Yellow	Salmon pink	Amber
7. Netzach	Amber	Green	Yellow green	Olive flecked with gold
8. Hod	Violet	Orange	Brick red	Yellowish black, flecked with white
9. Yesod	Indigo	Violet	Dark purple	Citrine, flecked with azure
10. Malkuth	Yellow	Citrine, olive, russet, black	Citrine, olive, russet, black, flecked with gold	Black, rayed with yellow

* The Briatic or Queen Scale is used by Kabbalists in their magic rituals. For example, if the magician is doing a ritual for love he has to work with the sphere of Netzach, whose color is green in the Briatic scale. That means that the magician should surround himself with the color green during the ritual, and visualize this color vibration around him as he works.

TABLE 5   Correspondences in the Tree of Life

Sephiroth	Planet	Physical Correspondence	Symbols	Magical Image	Virtue	Vice
1. Kether	First swirlings	Cranium	Point, Swastika	Bearded king in profile	Attainment	—
2. Chokmah	Zodiac	Left side of face	Phallus, straight line	Bearded male	Devotion	—
3. Binah	Saturn	Right side of face	Cup, Female Sex Organs	A matron	Silence	Avarice
4. Chesed	Jupiter	Left arm	Orb, Tetra-hedron	Crowned and Throned King	Obedience	Tyranny
5. Geburah	Mars	Right arm	Pentagon, Sword	Warrior in his chariot	Courage	Destruction
6. Tiphareth	Sun	Breast	Cube	Majestic King, a Child	Devotion to the Great work	Pride
7. Netzach	Venus	Loins, Hips, Legs	Rose, Lamp and Girdle	Lovely naked woman	Unselfish-ness	Lust
8. Hod	Mercury	Loins, Legs	Names, Versicles and Apron	Hermaphrodite	Truthful-ness	Dishonesty
9. Yesod	Moon	Reproductive organs	Perfumes, Sandals	Beautiful naked man	Independ-ence	Idleness
10. Malkuth	Earth, 4 elements	Feet, Anus	Equal-armed Cross	Young Woman, crowned and throned	Discrimina-tion	Inertia

151

mony is nullified and the power invoked is dispersed and returns whence it came. If the Kabbalist is working with a positive force for a noble purpose, or if the ritual is intended to benefit him or someone else, without harming anyone, there is nothing to fear, for the force invoked is a pure, Divine essence. If, however, he is laboring for the purpose to harm someone or to cause any form of destruction, the force that he has failed to "earth," which is Qliphotic in principle, can spread its evil tentacles around him and can easily destroy him.

One of the things that the practicing Kabbalist must bear in mind when he is doing practical work on the Tree is that the sephiroth work in pairs. Thus if he wishes to contact the sphere of Netzach on the right-hand pillar, he must remember to establish a link with the sphere of Hod, on the left-hand pillar. This way he is working with a pair of opposites, which is, as we have seen, the principle upon which the universe was created. If he fails to do this, he throws the entire Tree out of balance, giving rise to the chaotic forces of the Qliphoth, which are always lurking in the background of every magical ceremony.

The reason why the magical system of the Practical Kabbalah is known as the "Flash of Lightning" is that

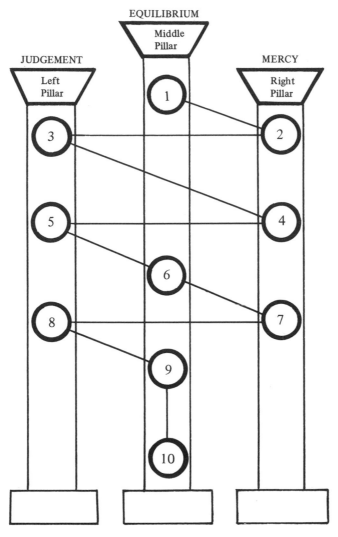

Fig. 7   The Flash of Lightning or Descent of Power

153

the Sephiroth emanate each other in a zig-zag form (see Fig. 3, p. 102).

Another system that uses the Flash of Lightning as a working method is that known by occultists as "rising on the planes." By means of this system the Kabbalist elevates his consciousness by contacting the various sephiroth. For this purpose he "travels astrally" over the different Paths that connect the sephiroth.

As a practical system the Tree of Life is of immense value, not only to the magician, but also to anyone who desires to harmonize the cosmic forces that form the structure of his soul. For we must remember that each sephira represents the purest essence of a human quality or virtue. If we absorb the Tree into our souls, we are harmonizing ourselves with the Divine aspects of these qualities and virtues. This is the highest and purest aim of practical work on the Tree of Life.

8 The Nature of the Soul

The Soul of Man

Before man's soul was manifested in the World of Action, it was in a state of nonexistence ("oyin"). That is, it was blended with the Infinite Light. After the Light became "restricted," and issued the World of Emanation, the soul assumed the form of "yesh me-oyim," which is existence from nonexistence. This means that the soul is in reality a part of God, for it originates in the Infinite Light.

According to the Kabbalistic doctrine, the nature of the soul is fivefold. The first two divisions are archetypal in essence and thus transcend man's ability to understand or even to conceive of them. They are called Yechida and Chaya and correspond respectively to the World of Adam Kadmon and the World of Emanation. The next three divisions are the three "elements" of the soul. The first of these is called Neshamah (the Higher Self), and comprises the first sephiroth of the Tree of Life—Crown, Wisdom, and

Understanding. It resides in the brain. The second is known as Ruach (Spirit), which comprises the next six sephiroth of the Tree, from Mercy to Foundation. Its seat is in the heart. The last one is Nephesch (Lower Nature), to which is assigned the last sephira, Kingdom. It resides in the liver. Neshamah is the source, the intelligence or knowledge; Ruach is the incentive to action; and Nephesch is the power of life that gives movement to the members of the body. Thus every act must start in the brain (Neshamah), be transmitted to the heart (Ruach), and finally to the organs that bring the act to completion (Nephesch) because the body by itself has no volition or power to move. Ruach or the "heart" in this Kabbalistic concept is the power of the will. Because the soul is an "offspring of the Heavenly Man (Adam Kadmon)" it is also called Adam or "man," while the body is called the "flesh of man." Therefore the *real man* is the soul and not the body.

The three degrees of the soul are also assigned by the Kabbalists to the three pillars of the Tree of Life, where Neshamah represents the Pillar of Mercy, Ruach corresponds to the Pillar of Judgment, and Nephesch is the Middle Pillar. Neshamah is also seen as the representation of Kether, the first sephira of the Tree, which is the "highest state of being." Ruach is then seen as Tiphareth, which is placed in the center of the Middle Pillar and corresponds to the heart in the human body, or the moral world. Lastly, Nephesch is assigned to Malkuth, the seat of the animal instincts and desires, known as the material or sensuous world.

Interestingly enough these three divisions of the "soul" according to the Kabbalistic doctrine can be equated with the Jungian concepts of the *Self*, the *Psyche*, and the *Shadow*. The reason for the distinct correspondences between these Jungian concepts and the Kabbalistic degrees of the soul may be found in Jung's lifetime interest in occult matters, notably the alchemical sciences. It is a well-known fact that Alchemy bears a strong correlation with the Kabbalah, and one of the most significant works on the Kabbalistic concepts is the Aesch Metzareph, which is a "chymico-Kabbalistic" treatise almost entirely alchemical in its teachings. The principal aim of the Aesch Metzareph is to assign the various sephiroth of the Tree of Life to the alchemical principles and metals. Since Jung is known to have read practically every

157

alchemical treatise in existence, it is reasonable to assume that he was acquainted with the Aesch Metzareph, and thus with the Kabbalistic doctrines.

The first degree of the soul, according to the Kabbalah, is Neshamah, the highest state of consciousness, also identified with Kether, the first emanation of the Infinite Light. It is comparable with Jung's concept of the Self. But the term "Self" is not used by Jung in the ordinary sense of the word, but rather in the Eastern manner, where the Self is conceived of as the "Supreme Being," the sum and total of all things, the "substance" of being. To Jung this concept of the Self is not universal consciousness, which is also known as the "unconscious." It is rather "an awareness on one hand of our unique natures, and on the other of our intimate relationship with all life, not only human, but animal and plant, and even that of inorganic matter and the cosmos itself." The Self, says Jung, "is not only the centre but also the whole circumference which embraces both conscious and unconscious." In Kabbalistic terms, it is the point within a circle and the circle itself. It is All that man may be and the totality of all possible knowledge, both conscious and unconscious. It is Neshamah.

The second degree of the soul, in Kabbalistic terms, is Ruach, equated with the heart or the "will." It is the centre of outward consciousness, where man becomes aware of thought forms and is able to mold thoughts into action. It is vastly similar to the Jungian concept of the *Psyche*, which is the mind and all mental activity on a conscious as well as on an unconscious level. According to Jung, the conscious mind "grows out of an unconscious psyche which is older than it, and which goes on functioning together with it or even in spite of it." Everything made by man had its beginnings in the Psyche; it was something he "thought about" and thus molded into action. The mental energy that gives rise to thoughts that are then brought into action was called *Libido* by Jung, and it does not have an exclusively sexual meaning as in Freudian psychology, but has the "general sense of desire, longing, urge." It may be comparable to the "etheric" substance of Yesod, the lunar sephira that is the last component of the Ruach, and in which, according to Kabbalists, thoughts are molded before they become actualized in the World of Action. To Jung, the Psyche is a system that is dynamic, constantly moving and self-regulating. It is interesting to note that in this

Jungian concept of the Psyche, the natural movement of the libido, or psychic energy, is forward and backward like the "movement of the tides." This is a clear correspondence with the lunar forces of Yesod, which is in the Ruach. To Jung, all human experience is psychic in principle. In *The Basic Postulates of Analytical Psychology*, he stated:

All that I experience is psychic. Even physical pain is a psychic image which I experience; my sense-impressions—for all that they force upon me a world of impenetrable objects occupying space—are psychic images, and these alone constitute my immediate experience, for they alone are the immediate objects of my consciousness. My own psyche even transforms and falsifies reality, and it does this to such a degree that I must resort to artificial means to determine what things are like apart from myself. Then I discover that a sound is a vibration of air of such and such a frequency, or that a color is a wave of light of such and such a length. We are in truth so wrapped about by psychic images that we cannot penetrate at all to the essence of things external to ourelves. All our knowledge consists of the stuff of the psyche which, because it alone is immediate, is superlatively real. Here, then, is a reality to which the psychologist can appeal—namely, psychic reality.

If the Ruach is "psychic reality," the Nephesch or Lower Nature is the Jungian concept of the *Shadow.* This term is used by Jung to define what he called "the personal unconscious," that is, those instincts and desires that are against society and our "ideal personality." But, as he also pointed out, there is no shadow without the sun, or some form of light. Thus the shadow may be seen as the dark side of the consciousness that resides in the "sun center of Tiphareth," in the Ruach, or human mind. The Shadow may be also equated with the dark forces of the Qliphoth, which are forever lurking in the background of every human action.

According to the Kabbalah, souls are androgynous in their original state, that is, they are bisexual in nature. When they descend to the material world, they separate into male and female and inhabit different bodies. If, during their mortal lives, the two halves of the soul meet, a great attachment develops between them, and thus it is said that through their marriage, or union, they become again conjoined. This is the source of the term "soul mates." This concept also

161

finds a correspondence in the Jungian school, in the dual idea of "animus and anima." The "anima" is the unconscious of a man, containing a complementary feminine counterpart, while the "animus" is the woman's unconscious, with masculine characteristics. Jung stated that "an inherited collective image of woman exists in a man's unconscious, with the help of which he apprehends the nature of a woman." The same is true of a woman in relation to a man's nature. That is the reason why it is so common to find both masculine and feminine characteristics in one person.

The Evil Spirit

According to the Kabbalah, when They created the Qliphoth, or evil beings, the Creators intended that in the material world there would be a power of evil that would necessitate choice on the part of man in order that he might be again united with the Infinite Light. It is almost as if there was a dual quality to God's nature, half of which is good and half of which is "evil." It may then be conceived that the Deity, by manifesting Themselves through man, intended, not to anihilate this "evil" or negative aspect, but rather to harmonize it and equilibrate it with the positive or "good" aspect. This is the eternal struggle in man's soul over "good" and "evil." For in man the consciousness of the atom becomes manifest. Man is "aware." He *knows* he is. To use René Descartes' famous statement, *Cogito, ergo sum* ("I think, therefore I am"). For man is not just a part of God, he *is* God on a lower, material level. Just as a photon is a unit of light, not a "part" of light, but light itself with all of light's qualities and attributes. The Kabbalah states that "all multiplicity, all defects and all judgements arise from the Ain Soph." The question of how could multiplicity and defects be derived from the Ain Soph, which is both Unity and Perfect Purity, is answered by the Kabbalists with the concept of "yesh me-oyin," that is, existence from nonexistence. The Infinite Light, since It has within Itself the hidden seed of all future manifestations, has also the latent power to create "evil" as well as "good."

The ten sephiroth of the Tree of Life, as we have already seen, have four stages of "light differentiation," which are called the Four Worlds of the Kabbalists, and which correspond to the four elements of the alchemists. The ten adverse sephiroth, or Qliphoth, have also four divisions, which correspond to

163

four "negative" elements. These four Qliphotic elements are present in man as follows:

1. Negative fire—arrogance
2. Negative air—superfluous talk
3. Negative water—cupidity
4. Negative earth—melancholy

According to Rabbi L. I. Krakovsky,

the element of water in the world of shell (Qliphoth) is called 'proud waters.' In man this is the white fluid or lymph which is the source of his phlegmatic states. This power seduces man to iniquity. In the source it is called the great cloud. The second element is the element of fire which burns the world in its flame and from it is also derived the fire of hell. In man it is the gall which embitters the world with its bitterness. In the origin it is called a flashing fire. The third element is air, or wind. It is a whirlwind from out of the north which stirs up the entire world. The fourth element is that of earth, the black earth, the dry, the empty.

The dual concept of "good" and "evil," which is represented so vividly by the Kabbalah in the glyphs of the Tree of Life and the Qliphoth, can be seen in the worlds of matter and "antimatter." As early as 1930, physicists had postulated that for each atomic particle an "antiparticle" ought to exist. That meant that the negatively charged electron should have as equivalent an antielectron with similar properties, except for the possession of a positive charge of the same size as the electron's negative charge. The same would be true of a negatively charged proton, in contrast with the actual proton, which is positively charged. The neutron, which is uncharged, would have its equivalent in an "antineutron" with a magnetic field oriented in the opposite direction to that of the regular neutron. Although this theory seemed farfetched at first, in 1932, the American physicist Carl D. Anderson discovered the "antielectron," which we know today familiarly as the positron. The "antiproton" and the "antineutron" were discovered in 1956. These discoveries led to further speculations among physicists and astrophysicists who argued that at the time of the explosion of the "cosmic egg" a particle and an antiparticle must have been formed. This theory was finally actualized by Austrian-American physicist Maurice Goldhaber, who has suggested the possibility of the existence of a Universe of matter and an Anti-Universe of antimatter, which he calls "cosmon" and "anticosmon," respectively.

This duality of nature, so evident throughout the created universe, has been termed by Jung "the opposites." The action of these "opposites" is linked by the Jungian school to the positive and negative poles of an electric circuit, or to the diastole and systole movement of the heart. The greater the tension between two opposites, the greater the energy that will be derived. According to Jung, "without opposition there is no manifestation of energy." The list of opposites that can be cited is endless. Among them, there are progression and regression, extraversion and introversion, thinking and feeling, and so on, ad infinitum.

The cosmic energy in man, what Jung called psychic energy and which manifests itself perennially in the form of two diametrically opposed principles, has its seat in the "libido." Since the libido is natural energy, its principal purpose is to serve the principles that govern life and the creation, but because of its "plastic" quality it can be used also for creative purposes. According to the Jungian school, "this direction of energy becomes initially possible by transferring it to something similar in nature to the object of instinctive interest." This is what is called "magic" in the practical Kabbalah. But it is in itself a completely nattural act because all it necessitates is the strong will of man and his vehement desire to bring his thought forms into actual realization. In this sense man is simply using the divine spark that is in him to bring about an Act of Creation.

Throughout our discussion of the Kabbalistic doctrine, we have seen how it is permeated with the concept of two opposites united for the purpose of manifestation. From proton and electron to man and woman, all the mysteries of creation are explained by the Kabbalah with this intensely sexual philosophy. To the Kabbalist, all the various degrees of manifestation are reduced to the essential Kabbalistic equation: "The pulsation of life-death which is Aleph, latent existence, personified in the name AHIH (Eheieh), perennially emanates IHVH (Jehovah), with whom It unites for the purpose of creation." Thus, in the Kabbalistic view, the Act of Creation was essentially an Act of Love. And, since according to the established laws of physics, the Universe renews itself continuously throughout eternity, we can say with reasonable certainty that God *ARE* well, and alive and forever loving.

Bibliography

Achad, Frater. *Q.B.L.* New York, 1969.

Agrippa, Cornelius. *De Occulta Philosophia.* New York, 1971.

Anderson, P. R. *Science in Defense of Liberal Religion.* London, 1933.

Anon. *The Golden Verses of the Pythagoreans.* London.

Aristotle. *Metaphysics.* R. Hope, trans. New York, 1952.

Ashlag, I. L., Rabbi. *The Kabbalah, A Study of the Ten Illuminations of Rabbi Isaac Luria.* Israel, 1971.

Aude, Sapere. *The Chaldean Oracles of Zoroaster.* New York.

Asimov, I. *The Universe.* New York, 1966.

Belchem, R. F. K. *A Guide to Nuclear Energy.* New York, 1958.

Best, Shabaz Britten. *Genesis Revised.* London, 1964.

Bible, The. *Genesis.*

Brill, A. A., ed. *The Basic Writings of Sigmund Freud.* New York, 1938.

Boehme, Jacob. *The Signature to All Things.* London, 1969.

Child, J. M. *The Early Mathematical Manuscripts of Leibniz.* London, 1920.

Cuny, H. *Albert Einstein.* New York, 1965.

Darwin, C. R. *The Origin of Species.* London.

d'Olivet, Fabre. *La Langue Hébraïque Restituée.* Paris.
    The Hebraic Tongue Restored. N. Redfield, trans. New York.

Durant, W. *The Story of Philosophy.* New York, 1953.

Fortune, Dion. *The Mystical Qabalah.* London, 1935.

Bibliography

Franck, A., *The Kabbalah*. London.

Gaer, J. *How the Great Religions Began*. New York, 1954.

Gamow, G. *The Creation of the Universe*. New York.

Ginsburg, C. D. *The Kabbalah*. London, 1863.

Hall, C. S. A. *A Primer of Freudian Psychology*. New York, 1954.

Huxley, Aldous. *The Perennial Philosophy*. New York, 1962.

Jung, C. G. *The Archetypes and the Collective Unconscious*. New York, 1959.
> *The Structure and Dynamics of the Psyche*. New York, 1960.
> *Mysterium Coniunctionis*. New York, 1963.

Kant, I. *Prolegomena to Any Future Metaphysics*. New York, 1951.

Knight, G. *A Practical Guide to Kabbalistic Symbolism*. London, 1965.

Krakovsky, L. I. Rabbi. *Kabbalah, The Light of Redemption.* Israel, 1970.

Leibniz, W. *Monadology*. London, 1890.

Lully, R. *The Tree of Love*. E. Allison Peers, transl. London, 1926.

Luzzato, M. C., Rabbi. *General Principles of the Kabbalah*. New York, 1970.

Mathers, S. L. MacGregor. *The Kabbalah Unveiled*. New York, 1971.

Myer, I. *Qabbalah*. New York, 1970.

Ouspensky, P. *Tertium Organum, A Key to the Enigmas of the World*. New York, 1968.

Plato, *Phaedo*. B. Jouet, transl. New York, 1942.

Progoff, I. *Jung, Synchronicity and Human Destiny*. New York, 1973.

Regardie, I. *A Garden of Pomegranates*. Minnesota, 1970.
> *The Tree of Life*. New York, 1972.

Russell, B. *The ABC of Relativity*. London, 1958.

Bibliography

Scholem, G. *Major Trends in Jewish Mysticism.* New York, 1954.

      On the Kabbalah and Its Symbolism. New York, 1965.

Suarés, C. *The Cipher of Genesis.* Berkeley, 1970.

Trachtenberg, J. *Jewish Magic and Mysticism.* New York, 1961.

Voltaire. *Philosophical Dictionary* (See Genesis). Besterman, T., ed. Middlesex, England, 1971.

Waite, A. E. *The Holy Kabbalah.* New York, 1960.

Westcott, W. W., ed. *The Sepher Yetzirah, The Book of Formation.* London.

      Aesch Mezareph or The Purifying Fire. New York.

Zohar, The Book of Splendour. G. Scholem, ed. New York, 1949.